Sports Law in Uganda

Sports Law in Uganda

Prossy Namuga

This book was originally published as a monograph in the International Encyclopaedia of Laws/Sports Law.

Founding Editor: Roger Blanpain
General Editor: Frank Hendrickx
Volume Editor: Michele Colucci

Wolters Kluwer

Published by:
Kluwer Law International B.V.
PO Box 316
2400 AH Alphen aan den Rijn
The Netherlands
E-mail: lrs-sales@wolterskluwer.com
Website: www.wolterskluwer.com/en/solutions/kluwerlawinternational

Sold and distributed by:
Wolters Kluwer Legal & Regulatory U.S.
7201 McKinney Circle
Frederick, MD 21704
United States of America
E-mail: customer.service@wolterskluwer.com

ISBN 978-94-035-0056-0

e-Book: ISBN 978-94-035-4815-9
web-PDF: ISBN 978-94-035-4825-8

The Author

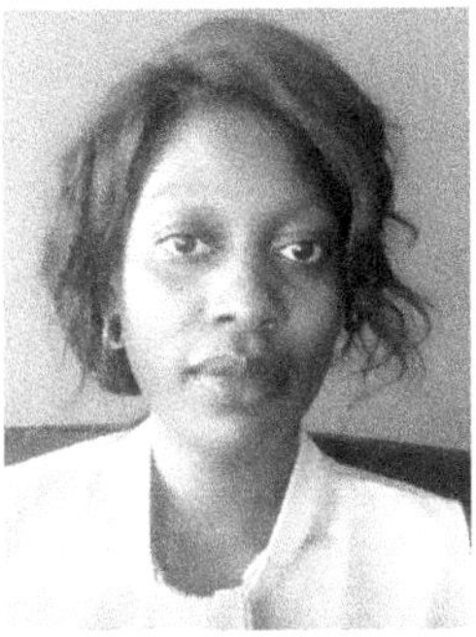

Prossy Namuga is an Advocate of the High Court of Uganda. She is a holder of a Bachelor of Laws (Hons) Degree, LLB from Makerere University, Kampala, Uganda and a Postgraduate Diploma in Legal Practice from the Law Development Center, Kampala, Uganda. She is a Legal Practitioner and a member of the Uganda Law Society and East African Law Society.

The Author

Table of Contents

Table of Contents

List of Abbreviations

AIBA	International Boxing Association
AUUS	Association of Uganda University Sports
CECAFA	Council for East and Central Africa Football Associations
CGF	Common Wealth Games Federation
FIFA	International Federation of Association Football
FMU	Federation of Motor Sports Associations of Uganda
FUBA	Federation of Uganda Basketball Associations
FUFA	Federation of Uganda Football Association
IOC	International Olympic Committee
KFU	Kabaddi Federation of Uganda
NCS	National Council of Sports
PAU	Pool Association of Uganda
PAYE	Pay As You Earn
UAF	Uganda Athletics Federation
UAF	Uganda Archery Federation
UBASA	Uganda Baseball and Softball Association
UCA	Uganda Cricket Association
UCF	Uganda Chess Federation
UDA	Uganda Draughts Association
UDBF	Uganda Dragon Boat Federation
UFA	Uganda Floorball Association
UFA	Uganda Football Association
ULA	Uganda Lacrosse Association
UOC	Uganda Olympic Committee
URA	Uganda Roll Ball Association
URF	Uganda Rowing Federation
URU	Uganda Rugby Union
USF	Uganda Swimming Federation
UVF	Uganda Volleyball Federation

List of Abbreviations

Acknowledgements

I thank my husband, Elias. From reading early drafts of this monograph to reviewing the final versions, he was as important to this monograph getting done as I was. Am grateful.

Acknowledgements

General Introduction

§1. General Background

1. Uganda is a sovereign country that lies in East Africa and is land locked. It is bordered by South Sudan in the North, Kenya in the East, Democratic Republic of Congo in the West and Rwanda and Tanzania in the South.[1] Geographically, Uganda is largely covered by a plateau although it has a couple of mountains, which include Mt. Rwenzori, Moroto and Elgon. It is also covered with a number of water bodies like Lake Victoria, which is the largest fresh water lake in Africa and second largest in the world, Lake Edward, Lake George, Lake Albert and Lake Kyoga.[2] Uganda is similarly the source of the River Nile, which is the longest river in the world.[3]

2. Uganda is a Republic, and it achieved this status on 9 October 1962 when the country attained independence from British colonial rule.[4] Uganda is a multi-lingual Republic composed of fifty-six indigenous communities who speak different languages.[5] Given that Uganda was a British colony, the English legal system and law are predominant; its legal system is thus based on English common law and customary law. However, customary law is in effect only when it does not conflict with statutory law.[6] The laws applicable in Uganda are statutory law, common law, doctrines of equity and customary law.[7] The Constitution is the supreme law in Uganda and any law or custom that is in conflict with it is null and void to the extent of the inconsistency.[8]

3. The *African Union Policy Framework for the Sustainable Development of Sport in Africa (2008–2018)* defines 'Sports' as a physical activity that is governed by a set of rules or customs involving specific administration, governing bodies,

1. BBC News, *Uganda Country Profile*, 10 May 2018. Available at: https://www.bbc.com/news/world-africa-14107906 (Accessed 5 Jan. 2022).
2. Country Reports, Uganda Geography. Available at: https://www.countryreports.org/country/Uganda/geography.htm (Accessed 5 Jan. 2022).
3. Traci Pedersen, The Nile: Longest River in the World Live Science, 30 Nov. 2016. Available at: https://www.livescience.com/57023-nile-river-facts.html (Accessed 5 Jan. 2022).
4. BBC News, *Uganda Country Profile*, 10 May 2018. Available at: https://www.bbc.com/news/world-africa-14107906 (Accessed 5 Jan. 2022).
5. Schedule 3 of the Constitution of the Republic of Uganda, 1995.
6. Article 2 of the Constitution of the Republic of Uganda, 1995.
7. The Judicature Act, Laws of Uganda.
8. Article 2 of the Constitution of the Republic of Uganda, 1995.

organizations often engaged in competitively.[9] Traditionally, Ugandans participated in sports activities like Omweso which is more of a board game that was supposedly introduced by the Bachwezi people of the ancient Bunyoro Kitara Empire of Uganda. They also engaged in wrestling.

4. With a national league and yearly playoffs, soccer is the most popular sport and spectator entertainment in Uganda. Cricket and rugby also attract large number of spectators. Uganda also sends athletes to the world's main sporting events, especially the Olympics.

5. The sports sector in Uganda has an obsolete perception that it is a leisure activity. Sports world over has transcended the leisure tag to become one of the most lucrative commercial ventures, paying the highest in wages and bonuses to athletes. However, in Uganda, sports remains tied to the ancient umbilical cord of leisure, which makes it difficult to advance the sector, harness its immense potential and reap from it.[10] In an effort to mainstream sports in Uganda, the former Speaker of the Parliament of Uganda, Rt. Hon. Rebecca Kadaga called for a Bill that will make sports compulsory in all institutions around the country. The Speaker made these remarks while launching the Monthly Parliamentary outdoor health and fitness sessions on Thursday, 28 June 2018. She was quoted to have said that:

> Our health is very important so we need to safeguard it by exercising regularly and that is why we have launched this exercise regimen to be carried out every Month.[11]

§2. Sources of Sports Law

6. Uganda has been a common law State since it inherited British common law. From the time when independence was obtained in 1962, attempts are being made to enact laws with domestic cultural values and aspirations of the people of Uganda. There exists an anachronistic national law governing the regulation and management of sports in Uganda.[12] Whereas there cannot be a single legislation to regulate sports given the various areas of its outreach, tort, tax, contract, employment, intellectual property law, constitutional law, commercial law, administrative law, it is imperative that the administrative and constitutional aspects are dealt with in a 'one-stop' law to avoid ambiguity. Most international sports bodies, International Federation of Association Football (FIFA), International Olympic Committee (IOC),

9. African Union Policy Framework for the Sustainable Development of Sport in Africa (2008–2018). Available at: https://au.int/sites/default/files/pages/32902-file-final_sport_policy_framework_for_africa-version_to_be_printed_-_english.pdf. (Accessed 5 Jan. 2022).
10. Daily Monitor, 'Stakeholders want Sports Redefined' 25 May 2020 accessed 4 Jul. 2021. Available at: https://www.monitor.co.ug/uganda/sports/other-sport/stakeholders-want-sports-redefined-1891622.
11. Parliament of Uganda, 'Speaker Calls for a bill on Compulsory Sports.' 28 Jun. 2018 https://www.parliament.go.ug/news/2030/speaker-calls-bill-compulsory-sports (Accessed 6 Jan. 2022).
12. Mulema Mukasa, Impact of Sports Betting and Corruption: Reflections from Uganda, 29 Nov. 2012.

International Association of Athletics Federations (IAAF) usually pay respect to the national laws in regard to the establishment and affiliation of the national associations and peaceful coexistence so long as there is no political interference in the management of national associations by the State.

7. There are five sources of sports law in Uganda and these include:

The Constitution of the Republic of Uganda, 1995. This is the supreme law of the land and all other laws must conform to it. In the event that any law is inconsistent, the Constitution of the Republic of Uganda, 1995 takes precedence.[13] The Constitution of the Republic of Uganda, 1995 does not point out specific rights to sports expressly. However, it provides that even those rights that are not specifically mentioned in the Constitution be observed:

> ... The rights, duties, declarations and guarantees relating to the fundamental and other human rights and freedoms specifically mentioned in this Chapter shall not be regarded as excluding others not specifically mentioned ... [14]

The Constitution of the Republic of Uganda, 1995 contains principles, which adjudicate the respective rights of parties involved in the sports world. The National Objectives and Directive Principles of State Policy in the Constitution of the Republic of Uganda, 1995 provide that the State shall promote recreation and sports for the citizens of Uganda.[15] This is aimed at protecting the rights of the athletes. Similarly, constitutional provisions also regulate bad conduct of the athletes, such as drug abuse, gender discrimination, racial segregation, since it is forbidden under the Constitution of the Republic of Uganda, 1995. The Constitution provides that all persons are equal before the law in all spheres of political, economic, social and cultural life and in every other respect and shall enjoy equal protection of the law.[16] The Constitution of the Republic of Uganda, 1995 goes on to indicate that a person shall not be discriminated against on the ground of sex, race, colour, ethnic origin, tribe, birth, creed or religion, social or economic standing, political opinion or disability.[17] The Constitution of the Republic of Uganda, 1995 also highlights that to 'discriminate' means to give different treatment to different persons attributable only or mainly to their respective descriptions by sex, race, colour, ethnic origin, tribe, birth, creed or religion, social or economic standing, political opinion or disability.[18] The Constitution of the Republic of Uganda, 1995 indicates that everyone has a right to freedom of association, which shall include the freedom to form and join associations or unions, including trade unions and political and other civic

13. Article 2 of the Constitution of the Republic of Uganda, 1995.
14. Article 45 of the Constitution of the Republic of Uganda, 1995.
15. National Objective and Directive Principles of State Policy, Directive XVII.
16. Article 21 of the Constitution of the Republic of Uganda, 1995.
17. Article 21(2) of the Constitution of the Republic of Uganda, 1995.
18. Article 21 (3) of the Constitution of the Republic of Uganda, 1995.

organizations.[19] Therefore, such provisions within the Constitution of the Republic of Uganda, 1995 greatly intertwine with the sporting activities and must be observed by sportsmen/women in Uganda.

Legislation. Chapter six of the Constitution of the Republic of Uganda, 1995 establishes the legislative arm of government – Parliament, which is mandated to make laws on any matter for the peace, order, development and good governance of Uganda.[20] Legislation may also be referred to as Statutes, Acts of Parliament, Promulgations or Decrees. Parliament may also delegate its law-making powers to other bodies; for instance, to a District Local Council, a City Council, a Municipal Council of a Sub-County Local Council or a government official, such as a Minister. These bodies or persons with delegated legislative powers make laws referred to as bye-laws, ordinances, rules or regulations.[21] The law in Uganda governing sports is mainly the National Council of Sports Act, Cap 48 that was passed in 1964 and commenced on 25 June 1964.[22]

Case Law. The Courts of Law of Uganda apply the doctrine of precedent. This means that when deciding a case with facts similar to those of an earlier decided case, the courts decide the new case by following the principles of law set out in the earlier decision. The earlier decided cases are what are referred to as precedents. The courts of precedent are the Supreme Court, Court of Appeal and the High Court. Decisions of a higher court are binding while those of the same court are persuasive. A case in point is the High Court decision in *Legal Brains Trust Ltd v. Attorney General & Anor,*[23] in which the crux of the applicant's case was that Government cannot transform private sports associations into public sports bodies through the *National Council of Sports Regulations S. I. No. 38 of 2014.* The applicant in that case contended that doing so is a clear expropriation of property and a clear example of excessiveness of power, which is an illegal, irrational and unconstitutional purpose, sought to be achieved. The High Court of Uganda agreed with the applicant and granted a temporary injunction restraining the Government and National Council of Sports, their agents, servants, or any person from implementing or enforcing the *National Council of Sports Regulations S. I. No. 38 of 2014.*

Common Law and Doctrines of Equity. Common law and doctrines of equity are observed by virtue of following the English legal system. Common law refers to decisions of English judges, which were based on the customs of the English communities.[24] Equity means fairness. Other maxims of equity

19. Article 29(1) (e) of the Constitution of the Republic of Uganda, 1995.
20. Article 79(1) of the Constitution of the Republic of Uganda, 1995.
21. Section 38, Local Governments Act, CAP 243, Laws of Uganda.
22. Uganda Legal Information Institute. Available at: https://old.ulii.org/ug/legislation/consolidated-act/48 (Accessed 5 Jan. 2022).
23. Miscellaneous Application No.638 of 2014, [2014] UGHCCD 171. Available at: https://old.ulii.org/system/files/judgment/hc-civil-division/2014/171/hc-civil-division-2014-171.doc (Accessed 5 Jan. 2022).
24. A Citizen's Handbook on Law & Administration of Justice in Uganda, Third edition, Judicial Service Commission, (2007) p. 3.

include: he who comes to equity must come with clean hands, equity regards as done that which ought to be done, equity follows the law and delay defeats equity. Where the Ugandan laws do not provide a remedy, the common law and doctrines of equity are applied only if they are not contrary to Uganda's written law.

Customary Law. Customary law entails a number of customs followed by the different people of Uganda. Customary law is not written but entails the norms that are followed by people. For customary law to be followed, it must not be repugnant to natural justice and not contrary to the Constitution of the Republic of Uganda, 1995. It is highlighted in the Constitution of the Republic of Uganda, 1995 that cultural and customary values, which are consistent with fundamental rights and freedoms, human dignity, democracy and with the Constitution, may be developed and incorporated in aspects of Ugandan life.[25] The Constitution of the Republic of Uganda, 1995 outlawed criminal customary law in Uganda.

§3. Specificity of Sport

8. Sports in Uganda is a unique aspect. It is for the same reason that it has specific laws that seek to regulate it. Sports law represents nothing more than an amalgamation of various substantive areas of law that are relevant in the sports context. In line with this perspective, the term 'sports law' is a misnomer given that sports represent a form of activity and entertainment that is governed by the legal system in its entirety.[26] Sports law simply indeed entails the application of basic legal precepts to a specific industry that are drawn from other substantive areas of law.

9. Sports law can be seen as a concomitant of other substantive areas of law since it is in one way or another intertwined with other areas of law. This is because one cannot talk about 'sports law' without making reference to contract law, labour law, tort law and the Constitution of the Republic of Uganda, 1995. This notion therefore demonstrates the uniqueness of sports law among other areas of law since the sports industry in a broader sense covers various aspects like contracts, employment, agreements, violent fights, drug abuse etc., which are also of great interest within the legal sectors. In a nutshell, sports law with its wide variety of legal aspects probably encompasses more areas of law than other disciplines.

10. Overall, contract law retains a vitally important role in the business of sports. In Uganda, the *Contracts Act 2010* consolidates the law relating to contracts and agreements made between two or more people during their course of dealing. It is true that any amateur or experienced sports athlete who wishes to join a well-established sport club of any kind has to make what is termed as an 'enforceable contract' in order to legalize his/her consent and willingness to play for that club or

25. National Objective and Directive Principles of State Policy, Directive XXIV.
26. Timothy Davis, What Is Sports Law? *Marquette Sports Law Review*, Vol. 11, Issue 2 (2021) spring.

sports community.[27] Nevertheless, contract law principles retain their importance with respect to the interpretation and application of the terms of agreements between sports clubs and players that are open to individual negotiation. For example, in professional football, the following are provisions that are subject to individualized negotiation: the amount of signing, the time of payment, the length of the contractual relationship, skill or injury guarantees, salary adjustment agreements, roster bonuses and option clauses, among others.

27. Section 10, Contracts Act, 2010, Laws of Uganda.

Part I. The Legal Framework

Introduction

§1. Public Law and Fundamental Rights

I. Right to Practice Sport

11. The Constitution of the Republic of Uganda 1995 does not particularize the right to sports expressly like in other jurisdictions. However, the Constitution provides that the rights, duties, declarations and guarantees relating to the fundamental and other human rights and freedoms specifically mentioned in this chapter shall not be regarded as excluding others not specifically mentioned.[28] In Uganda, we can also impute the existence of rights that supporting sports to be a base of protection of sports. The Constitution obliges the State to provide recreation and sports avenues for the citizens of Uganda. This is enshrined in the National Objectives and Directive Principles of State Policy,[29] which provide that the State shall promote recreation and sports for the citizens of Uganda. For those who practice sport as an occupation in Uganda, the Constitution guarantees that every person in Uganda has the right to practice his/her profession and to carry on any lawful occupation, trade or business.[30]

II. Freedom of Association

12. Constitution of the Republic of Uganda, 1995 contains principles that adjudicate the respective rights of parties involved in the sports world. This is aimed at protecting the rights of the athletes. Uganda has made specific provisions for the right to freedom of association in its Constitution of the Republic of Uganda, 1995 thereby making it enforceable in its jurisdiction. The Constitution of the Republic of Uganda, 1995 recognizes the right of individuals to form and join associations or unions, including trade unions and political or other civic organizations.[31] Chapter four of the Constitution of the Republic of Uganda, 1995 provides that every person shall have the right to freedom of association, which shall include freedom to form

28. Article 45 of the Constitution of the Republic of Uganda, 1995.
29. Objective XVII of the Constitution of the Republic of Uganda, 1995.
30. Article 40(2) of the Constitution of the Republic of Uganda, 1995.
31. Constitution of the Republic of Uganda, 1995 of the Republic of Uganda, 1995, *supra* note 1.

and join associations, including trade unions and political and other civic organizations.[32] The Constitution of the Republic of Uganda, 1995 also provides that every Ugandan has a right to participate in peaceful activities to influence the policies of government through civic organizations.[33] Under the labour law, employees are free to join labour unions of their choice. This freedom is guaranteed under both the Constitution of the Republic of Uganda, 1995 and the Labour Unions Act. The Labour Unions Act also provides that employees shall have a right to organize themselves in any labour union and may assist in running the labour union, bargain collectively through a representative of their own choice, withdraw their labour and take industrial action.[34] Meanwhile, the employer is barred from interfering with this right to associate otherwise, if he/she does, he/she commits an offence for which he/she is criminally liable.[35]

13. Although the Constitution of the Republic of Uganda, 1995 provides for freedom of association, it indicates that this right is subject to the general limitations as provided in the same to the effect that in the enjoyment of one's rights and freedoms, a person must not prejudice the fundamental or other human rights and freedoms of others or act against the public interest.[36]

14. In *Charles Onyango Obbo and Anor. v. Attorney General,*[37] it was observed that associations should enjoy the freedom of association with only limitations that are acceptable and demonstrably justifiable in a free and democratic society. That Uganda as a democratic society must apply the universal standards of a democratic society.

15. In *Muwanga Kivumbi v. Attorney General,*[38] reference was made to the decision of the Supreme Court of Zimbabwe in *Mark Gova & Another v. Minister of Home Affairs & Another*[39] that pointed out a summary criterion for justification of laws that impose a limitation on guaranteed rights. To begin with, it was noted that the legislative objective which the limitation is designed to promote must be sufficiently important to warrant overriding a fundamental right. Second, the measures designed to meet the objective must be rationally connected to it and not arbitrary, unfair, or based on irrational considerations. Finally, the means used to impair the right or freedom must not be more than what is necessary to accomplish the objective.

16. These associations include sports associations such as Uganda Wrestling Federation, Uganda Dragon Boat Federation, Uganda Sport Climbing Association, Uganda Body Building and Fitness Association, Uganda Deaf Sports Federation,

---

32. *Ibid.*
33. Article 38(2) Constitution of the Republic of Uganda, 1995 of the Republic of Uganda, 1995.
34. Section 3 of the Labour Unions Act.
35. Section 5 of the Labour Unions Act.
36. Constitution of the Republic of Uganda, 1995 of the Republic of Uganda, *supra* note 5.
37. [Constitutional Petition No. 2 of 2002].
38. Constitutional Petition No. 9 of 2005, p.14.
39. [S.C.36/200: Civil Application No.156/99].

Uganda Boxing Federation, Federation of Uganda Basketball Associations (FUBA), Uganda Rugby Union (URU), Uganda Handball Federation, Uganda Chess Federation (UCF), Uganda Hockey Association, Uganda Athletics Federation (UAF), Uganda Netball Federation, Uganda Darts Association, Pool Association of Uganda (PAU), Uganda Kick Boxing Federation (UKBF), Uganda Tennis Association, Uganda Zurkhaneh Federation (UZF), Uganda Cycling Association, Uganda Floorball Association (UFA), Uganda Swimming Federation (USF), Gymnastics Association of Uganda, Uganda Archery Federation (UAF), Uganda Rowing Federation (URF), Uganda Table Tennis Association, Uganda Judo Association, Uganda Taekwondo Federation (UTF), Uganda Squash Rackets Association, Uganda Weightlifting Federation, Scrabble Association of Uganda, Uganda Ultimate Frisbee Association, Uganda Paralympic Committee (UPC), Uganda Wood ball Federation, Uganda Fencing Association (UFA), Uganda Canoe Kayak Federation, Association of Uganda University Sports (AUUS), Uganda Draughts Association (UDA), Uganda Baseball & Softball Association, Kabaddi Federation of Uganda (KFU), Uganda Ludo Association, American Football Association of Uganda, Uganda Lacrosse Association (ULA), Uganda Golf Union, Uganda Skating Federation, Uganda Roll Ball Association (URA), Uganda Volleyball Federation (UVF), Uganda Badminton Association, Uganda Cricket Association (UCA), Federation of Motor Sports Associations of Uganda (FMU) and Federation of Uganda Football Associations (FUFA).

III. Personality Rights

17. Image rights are the expression of personality in the public domain. In simple terms, these are personality rights. Under the common law jurisprudence, a personality right is the right of an individual to control the commercial use of his/her name, image, likeness, or other unequivocal aspects of one's identity.[40]

18. When it comes to personality rights, indeed in Uganda, there is no specific 'image rights' law as such, but these rights can be construed from other human rights enshrined under chapter four of the Constitution of the Republic of Uganda, 1995. This is simply because the legal regime as regards image rights has not been largely explored hence little jurisprudence from our jurisdiction both in statute and precedent. Even here in Uganda, although we do not have a legal regime that addresses image rights it does not mean persons who suffer wrongs cannot seek redress from courts.

19. Hon. Justice Peter Adonyo stated in *Asege Winnie v. Opportunity Bank (U) Ltd & Anor* that: 'The mere lack of a legal regime in our jurisdiction that addresses the question of image rights cannot be taken to mean that persons who suffer wrongs cannot seek redress from courts of law when in fact they are aggrieved.' It was observed in that case that personality rights include the right of publicity or to keep one's image and likeness from being commercially exploited without permission or

40. *Asege Winnie v. Opportunity Bank (U) Ltd & Anor High Court Civil Suit*No. 756 of 2013.

contractual compensation and the right to privacy, and the right to be left alone and not have one's personality represented publicly without permission.

20. Asege Winnie, the plaintiff in this matter was stated to be a successful commercial farmer based in Soroti District in Uganda. She brought the suit through her legal counsel against Opportunity Bank (U) Limited, which was the defendant in the matter for breach of her constitutional right to privacy, passing off, misrepresentation and false endorsement, breach of confidence and unjust enrichment in the unauthorized use of her image. She sought to recover 10% royalty fees for the use of her image at an interest rate of 22% from the date of cause of action until payment in full, general damages, aggravated damages, punitive damages and costs of the suit. Maad Limited, an advertising company, was added as a third party in these matters after it was stated that it was an agent of the defendant.

21. Asege operated under the name of Dakabela Rural Women Development Association in which she was chairperson. In 2013, she saw her image posted on a huge billboard run by the defendant in which she was shown to be heartily laughing and holding a bountiful harvest of oranges in her hands with a caption '*Save for your success with the Agro Save Account.*' In addition to those huge billboards, the defendant is stated to have produced advertising flyers, brochures and calendars bearing similar images of the plaintiff as those depicted in the huge billboards, which the defendant liberally distributed to its branches countrywide. The plaintiff states that these productions were never commissioned, assigned, licensed or prior consent granted to the defendant to take her photograph and put her image on the said billboards and such other publications. Thus, the defendant obtained the same without authority, grossly misused, and unjustifiably published her private information. This was an invasion of her constitutional right to privacy with the result that owing to the defendant's unauthorized use of her image, the plaintiff suffered substantial damages. It is for these reasons that she sought damages from the defendant who she believes did make substantial profits from the unauthorized use of her image for the illegal adverts that certainly attracted customers to open accounts with the defendant.

22. The defendant on the other hand denied the plaintiff's claim stating that in 2011 it engaged the services of the Maad Limited, which is an advertising company and third party. With these, they developed an advertising concept for its new product known as *Agro Save* with the third party developing the concept after advising it that the third party had lawfully purchased all the photographs used in the advertisement materials from an internet-based website known as Shutter Stock Inc. and from the New Vision Printing and Publishing Company Limited. Thus, consequently, the photographs, which were used, were lawfully acquired meaning that the plaintiff had no cause of action and therefore her suit should be dismissed with costs accordingly.

23. During the course of the proceedings, the defendant did file a third-party notice seeking to be indemnified by the third party against any liability brought against it by the plaintiff. When the third party came on board, it filed a written statement of defence in which it denied any liability over the alleged infringements of the rights of the plaintiff. The third party stated that the plaintiff did not and had no copyright over the photographs used by it for those photographs which it used were legally obtained from other entities and not the plaintiff. That in any case the person in the alleged photographs was not the plaintiff in any event and thus the plaintiff's claim should be dismissed with the contempt it deserves.

24. The adjudication of such rights is available to the sports fraternity in Uganda. A sports personality whose personality rights have been infringed can make a claim for violation of the right to privacy, passing off, false endorsement and unjust enrichment.

IV. Others

25. The legal framework governing sports in Uganda also embodies the equality rights for all sportsmen and women. The Constitution provides that all persons are equal before and under the law in all spheres of political, economic, social and cultural life and in every other respect and shall enjoy equal protection of the law.[41] The Constitution similarly indicates that no child shall be deprived by any person of medical treatment, education or any other social or economic benefit by reason of religious or other beliefs. This caters to the minors engaged in sports activities in Uganda.

26. Furthermore, sportsmen/women have the right to own property individually or collectively in the form of sports associations. The Constitution provides that every person has a right to own property either individually or in association with others.[42]

27. Uganda as a signatory to several international instruments, which provide for sport as a fundamental right, is obliged to protect the enjoyment of this right within its jurisdictions. Article 1 of the International Charter on Physical Education and Sport (1978) asserts the practice of physical education and sport as being a fundamental right for all: every human being has a fundamental right of access to physical education and sport. The same article stipulates that the freedom to develop physical, intellectual and moral powers through physical education and sport must be guaranteed both within the educational system and in other aspects of social life by the Member States. Article 24 of the UNDHR grants the right to rest and leisure, and Article 31 of the Convention on the Rights of a Child, 1990, recognizes the right of the child to rest and to enjoy leisure as well as engage in play and recreational activities. Article 30(5) of the Convention on the Rights of Persons with Disabilities (RPD) 2006 requires state parties to respond appropriately to enable persons with disabilities to participate on an equal basis with others in recreational, leisure and sporting activities.

---

41. Article 21(1) of the Constitution of the Republic of Uganda, 1995.
42. Article 26(1) of the Constitution of the Republic of Uganda, 1995.

§2. Governmental Conditions and Permits (Quotas, Work Restrictions)

28. Every national sports association in Uganda is required to be incorporated in accordance with the laws of Uganda,[43] or else the National Council of Sports cannot register it.[44] A sports association, which is not recognized by the Council, is restricted from using or referring to itself using 'Uganda'.[45] The National Council of Sports forbids registration of more than one national sports association in respect of each sport in Uganda.[46]

29. With regard to qualifications for participation in the governance of a national sports association, a person cannot hold an executive office of a national association unless that person has participated in the sport or been involved in the administration of the sport and is a citizen of Uganda. A person is deemed to have participated in the sport if he/she has played or participated in the sport in school at the district, regional, national or international level or if that person has been involved in the management or running of the sport at a level recognized by the Council.[47]

30. It is also forbidden for a person to hold an executive office or be involved, concurrently, in the governance of more than two national associations.

§3. Tax Law Applied to Sport

31. The main tax law that applies to sportsmen and women in Uganda is the Income Tax Act,[48] which requires that every employer shall withhold tax from a payment of employment income to an employee. This applies to sports personalities with employment contracts. Employment income consists of salary, allowances and benefits in kind. Income tax on employment income (commonly known as Pay As You Earn (PAYE)) is deducted by the employer from the employment income of every qualifying employee on a monthly basis and remitted to Uganda Revenue Authority.

32. Tax is imposed on the income derived in Uganda by every non-resident entertainer, sports person, or theatrical, musical or other related groups of entertainers. The tax is charged at a rate of 15% of the gross amount of the remuneration derived by the public entertainer/sports person. Where the tax is levied on a group, every member of the group is jointly and severally liable for payment of the tax. The obligation to withhold the tax under this provision is placed with the person

43. Regulation 3(1) the National Council of Sports Regulations, 2014.
44. Regulation 4(2) the National Council of Sports Regulations, 2014.
45. Regulation 11(1) of the National Council of Sports Regulations, 2014.
46. Regulation 4(3) of the National Council of Sports Regulations, 2014.
47. Regulation 7 of the National Council of Sports Regulations, 2014.
48. Section 116 of the Income Tax Act, CAP 340.

making the payment, e.g., promoter, agent, or such a similar person. The tax is payable before the person leaves the country.[49]

33. A person who makes payment for winnings of betting or gaming (sports betting or pool betting) is required to withhold tax (15%) on the gross amount of the payment.[50] Any agent paying remuneration to a non-resident sports person or responsible for collecting the gross receipts for a sports person must withhold from the remuneration or receipts a tax.

34. The sports agent who fails to withhold tax is personally liable to pay the Commissioner the amount of tax which has not been withheld and/or remitted to Uganda Revenue Authority. The agent, however, is entitled to recover the amount from the payee thereafter.[51]

35. Amateur sporting associations are exempt from income tax. An amateur sports association whose sole or the main object is to foster or control any athletic sport or game and whose members consist only of amateur sports persons or affiliated associations, with only amateur sports persons as members.[52] An award received by a sports person as a reward for winning or participating in a sports competition is exempted from taxation.[53]

36. The Lotteries and Gaming Act (Amendment) 2017[54] reduced the gaming tax from 35% to 20%.

37. Operators of a casino, gaming or betting activity issued with a licence are required, in addition to taxes prescribed by law, to pay a gaming tax.[55] All footballers who earn not less than UGX 230,000 (USD 62) a month pay 10% of it as PAYE to Uganda Revenue Authority.

§4. Principles of Tort Law

38. Tort law is the area of law that protects people from bad acts of others. When a person commits a tort, they violate law; for example, if a person suffers injury due to someone else's wrongful acts, the person who suffers the injury can bring a claim for compensation against that person who commits a tort. Therefore, tort law principles are applicable in sports settings as they apply in day-to-day life.

39. Weiler and Gary R. Roberts, in their book, *Sports and the Law*, state that:

---

49. *Ibid.*
50. Section 118C of the Income Tax Act CAP 340.
51. Section 116 of the Income Tax Act, CAP 340.
52. Section 2 of the Income Tax Act, CAP 340.
53. Section 21 of the Income Tax Act CAP 340.
54. Came into force on 13 Jun. 2017.
55. Section 48 of the Lotteries and Gaming Act, 2016.

Sports, however, pose a unique problem to the law of personal injury. The aim of a sporting event is to produce spirited athletic competition on the field or floor. In sports such as football, rugby, boxing etc., a central feature of the contest is the infliction of violent contact on the opponent. In other sports, such as basketball and baseball, such contact is an expected risk, if not a desired outcome of intense competition. Even sports such as golf, badminton, and tennis that are intrinsically nonviolent for their participants, may inflict harmful contacts upon the spectators. This characteristic feature of sports requires the law to undertake a delicate balancing act when it tailors for use in sports litigation the standards of liability developed to govern relationships in very different aspects of life.[56]

I. Civil Liability

40. Many sports activities pose serious dangers to sportsmen and women. Generally, a person who suffers a sports-related injury may recover medical expenses and other losses if the injury was caused by the negligence of another party. Injuries and damages resulting from intentional torts, such as a civil battery or civil assault, likewise are recoverable.

41. Assault and battery are intentional torts and thus can serve as the basis for a civil suit demanding compensation in the form of monetary damages, as was held in *Odiya Richard v. Okello John Bosco & Others.*[57] In this case, the appellant sued the respondents jointly and severally for recovery of general and special damages for personal injury, interest thereon and the costs of the suit. His claim was that on 7 September 2015, at Oryang Trading Centre, Lagoro Sub-County, Kitgum District, the respondents assaulted him thereby inflicting upon him actual bodily harm. As a result of that assault, he sustained: a deep incised wound (bite) on the side of his left hand, tenderness of the neck, strain in the limbs and multiple soft tissue injuries on various parts of his body. On medical examination, the injuries were classified as 'harm'. He reported the incident to the police whereupon the respondents were arrested, prosecuted and convicted of the offence of Assault Occasioning Actual Bodily Harm C/s 236 of *The Penal Code Act.* Each of them was sentenced to a fine UGX 500,000 or one year imprisonment in default. The appellant then filed the suit for recovery of UGX 2,200,000 in medical and related expenses, and UGX 450,000 per month from 7 September 2015 until the date of judgment as special damages for his lost income resulting from the loss of his job, consequent upon the injuries he suffered.

42. Proof of assault is on a balance of probabilities as was noted in *Mugwanya Patrick v. AG.*[58] In this case, the plaintiff claimed that on or about 15 December 2008, the plaintiff, in charge of Uganda Revenue Authority Security Eastern Region,

56. Weiler and Gary R. Roberts, 'Sports and the Law', Second edition, 1998, p. 240.
57. High Court Civil Appeal No. 45 of 2018.
58. High Court Civil Suit No. 154 of 2009.

received a report of theft of a Toyota Mark II Chassis No. GX 100-6051941 motor vehicle unit, which was unregistered and therefore numberless. The vehicle unit was still the property of Uganda Revenue Authority. The said motor vehicle was stolen from the park yard. After conducting investigations and acting on reasonable suspicion, he arrested the driver Abdullah of the missing motor vehicle Abdullah and its convoy leader Ali Kibwana who was then responsible for keeping the ignition keys for the stolen motor vehicle. Thereafter, the plaintiff handed over the two suspects to police officers at Malaba Police Station for more investigations and possible prosecution. To the plaintiff's surprise, the police released the two suspects without recording their statements and instead wrongfully arrested and locked him up on the same alleged offence of stealing a motor vehicle, and this was on the orders of the Officer in Charge of the station ASP Kyaligonza and the Officer in Charge CID Mr. Engungu and it was registered under Police CRB reference No. 359/08. Further, the plaintiff alleges that the Officer in Charge Station and Officer in Charge CID ordered the other detainees/suspects in the cells to beat up the plaintiff who sustained injuries in the process. That his detention in the circumstances was wrongful, malicious, deliberate, unjustified and false because it was not based on: any reasonable suspicion; it was intended to frustrate the plaintiff's effort to fight criminality done on Uganda Revenue Authority property because the missing motor vehicle has never been recovered; the plaintiff was detained for more than the statutory period. It is further contended that the Attorney General is vicariously liable for the actions of the policemen. After sustaining injuries the plaintiff incurred special damages of UGX 305,000 on account of paying for medical bills.

43. Under the law of limitations, a claim for assault must be filed within six years from the date it occurred.[59]

44. Courts generally decide suits involving injuries to athletes, spectators, and other parties involved in sports according to basic tort laws. If a party owes a duty of care towards another party and that duty is breached, the party owing the duty is liable for any injuries suffered by the party to whom the duty is owed that result from the breach. The level of care that must be exercised depends on the situation: dangerous situations require a high degree of care, whereas less dangerous situations require less care. Expectations may also play a part. For example, a spectator who is hit by a foul ball while sitting in the stands at a baseball stadium cannot recover for injuries because most fans know that stray balls in the stands are an inescapable by-product of baseball. However, a patron who is standing in the interior walkway of a stadium concourse may recover for injuries resulting from a foul ball. A spectator in the unfamiliar environs of a stadium is not aware of the dangers and thus is owed a greater duty of care by the baseball organization.

45. Athletes may recover for injuries resulting from another party's negligence or intentional acts. Liability for player-to-player conduct, where a player can sue another player in order to recover for injuries sustained if the other player 'intentionally struck, pushed, strangled etc.', him/her during the game, thus resulting in a

59. Section 3(1) of the Limitations Act Cap. 80.

tort. In both professional and amateur contact sports, athletes consent to some physical contact, but courts do not find that participants consent to contact that goes outside the bounds of the game.

46. Liability to fans. Under this, the sports club has to take the duty of care towards the fans regardless of whether they are invited or not. For example, if a player of a certain sports club attacks and injures a fan, the sports club is held liable for the injuries caused since it possesses the duty to protect the fans from any misconduct while watching the games. Another example is if the fans of the hosting sports club attack and cause injuries to the guest fans during a game, the sports club is held liable for not taking duty of care to protect the guests.

47. In some cases, schools may be held liable for injuries to athletes. The University may be held liable to student athletes. This can come about if there is negligence by the university sports management to take duty of care towards the sports athletes during practice, tournaments etc. Therefore, if any problem affects any player while under the university sports activities, the university is held liable for not taking duty of care, which is also a tort. If an employee of the school, such as a coach, teacher, or referee, fails to properly supervise a student and the student suffers an injury as a result of the failure in supervision, the school may be held liable for its employee's negligence. Generally, coaches, teachers, and referees must exercise reasonable care to prevent foreseeable injuries.

48. Medical malpractice. Here, a player can bring an action against the team and physicians for the fraudulent concealment of medical information whereby if a player gets an injury during the game and the team physician does not inform the player of the continuing risks associated with his injuries, and this can establish fraudulent concealment by the team which is also a tort.

49. In *Kabiito Telephorus v. Attorney General & Others,*[60] negligence was defined as the act of doing something or an omission by a reasonable man, guided upon considerations which regulate the conduct of human affairs. Further, in case of negligence there should be a duty of care owed, a breach of that duty and damage suffered by the person to whom the duty was owed. If a professional man possesses an art, he must reasonably be skilled in it. He must also be careful, but the standard of care, which the law requires, is not insurance against accidental slips.

50. In the aforementioned case of *Kabiito Telephorus*, the plaintiff brought the suit, as a husband of Katusabe Elizabeth alias E.G. Katusabe the deceased, on his own behalf and on behalf of the family for the benefit of the estate of the deceased under the Law Reform (Miscellaneous Provisions) Act. The plaintiff claimed special, general damages for negligence, unlawful death, loss of life, loss of dependency, care, pain and suffering, interest on damages at 26% per annum from the date of the cause action till payment in full and costs of the suit. The plaintiff founded his action in negligence. The particulars of negligence pleaded in the plaint were:

---

60. High Court Civil Suit No. 26 of 2012.

lack of proper medical attention towards the deceased who was in labour, failure by the defendant's workers to provide lifesaving blood, sill and equipment, leaving the deceased to bleed without rescue which resulted in her death, sheer and outright lack of care and indifference towards patients, poor health care standards in the first defendant's hospital, and lack of drugs and health facilities.

51. The defendants in sports-related personal injury suits may possess any number of defences. One of the most successful of these defences is that the party assumed the risk of being injured by playing in or watching the sporting event. The defendants may also argue that the plaintiff was negligent and therefore should recover only a portion of his damages or nothing at all. For example, a plaintiff may have ignored warnings or signed a document that waived the defendant's liability for any injury suffered by the plaintiff.

II. Criminal Liability

52. The main purpose of criminal liability is to enforce public justice. The Penal Code Act of Uganda provides for the criminal offence of common assault to wit: any person who unlawfully assaults another commits a misdemeanour, and, if the assault is not committed in circumstances for which a greater punishment is provided, is liable to imprisonment for one year.[61] The Penal Code Act also provides for assaults causing actual bodily harm to wit: any person who commits an assault occasioning actual bodily harm commits a misdemeanour and is liable to imprisonment for five years.

53. In *Uganda v. Okech and Anor*,[62] it was observed that for liability to arise in such offences, the following ingredients have to be proved: that the victim sustained grievous harm, the harm was caused unlawfully and the accused caused or participated in causing the grievous harm. Bodily 'harm' means any bodily hurt, disease or disorder whether permanent or temporary. The court in this case considered the nature of grievous harm as defined by section 2 (f) of the Penal Code Act as any harm which amounts to a maim or dangerous harm or seriously or permanently injures health or which is likely to injure health, or which extends to permanent disfigurement or to a permanent or serious injury to any external or internal organ, membrane or sense. The court noted that the differences between 'bodily harm' and 'grievous harm' therefore are: (1) in the case of grievous harm, the injury to health must be permanent or likely to be permanent, whereas to amount to bodily harm, the injury to health need not be permanent; (2) a mental injury may amount to grievous harm but not to bodily harm; (3) in order to amount to bodily harm, the physical injury must 'interfere with' health, whereas in the case of grievous harm, the injury must be 'of such a nature as to cause or be likely to cause' permanent injury to health.

61. Section 235 of the Penal Code Act, CAP 120.
62. [2019] Uganda High Court Criminal Division.

III. Public Health and Safety

54. The Constitution of the Republic of Uganda, 1995 provides that every person has a right to a clean and healthy environment.[63] In Uganda, the law that regulates health and safety at workplaces is the Occupational Safety and Health Act. Physical and psychological health is implied from the definition of bodily injury in the Occupational Safety and Health Act. The act states that 'bodily injury' includes injury to health. It further provides that it is the duty of a person who has control over premises to provide the safe means of access to and exit from the premises and to take measures that are reasonable to ensure that the premises remain safe without risk to health.[64] The Occupational Safety and Health Act defines an occupational disease as a disease contracted as a result of exposure to risk factors arising from a work activity.[65]

The Act spells out safety duties to employees (Sportsmen and women with contracts with sports associations) as discussed hereunder:

55. Duty to take reasonable steps to protect their own safety and health. Every employee has a duty to take reasonable care for the health and safety of himself/herself and of any other person who may be affected by hi/her actions or omissions at work.[66]

56. Self-employed persons' duty to take reasonable steps to protect their own and other people's health and safety. This applies to sportsmen and women who double as both the owners of the sports association and players for the same associations. Self-employed persons have a duty to conduct their undertakings in a way that ensures, as far as is reasonably practicable, that they and any other person who may be directly affected by their undertakings are not exposed to risks their health or safety.[67]

57. Duty to comply with OSH-related requirements. It is the duty of every worker while at work as regards any duty or requirements imposed upon the employer or, any other person, by or under statutory provision, to comply with the employer, as far as is necessary, to enable the duty or requirement to be performed or complied with.[68]

63. Article 39, Constitution of the Republic of Uganda, 1995.
64. Section 26, Occupational Safety and Health Act, 2006, Laws of Uganda.
65. Section 2, Occupational Safety and Health Act, 2006, Laws of Uganda.
66. Section 35(1)(a) Occupational Safety and Health Act, 2006.
67. Section 24 Occupational Safety and Health Act, 2006.
68. Section 35(1)(b) Occupational Safety and Health Act, 2006.

58. *Right to remove themselves from a dangerous situation.* A worker who moves himself/herself from a work situation which he or she has reasonable justification to believe presents an imminent and serious danger to his/her life shall not be punished or subjected to undue consequences, provided the danger is confirmed by the Commissioner.[69]

59. *Right to be reassigned to non-hazard work.* Where any assignment involves exposure to dangerous emissions or to substances and agents, which are harmful to health and is certified to be medically inadvisable to continue the exposure, it shall be the duty of the employer to provide the worker concerned with suitable alternative employment.

The Act also bestows the following obligations on employers (Sports Associations):

60. *Duty to ensure the health and safety of employees.* The employer is required to take, as far as is reasonably practicable, all measures for the protection of his/her workers and the general public from the dangerous aspects of the employer's undertaking at his/her cost.[70]

61. *Duty to protect the health and safety of people other than their own employees.* It is the duty of an employer to conduct his/her undertaking in a way that ensures, as far as is reasonably practicable, that any person, who is not his/her employee, but who may be affected by the undertaking, is not exposed to risks to his/her health and safety.[71]

62. *Collaboration among two or more employers at the same workplace.* Where two or more employers undertake activities simultaneously at one workplace, they shall have a duty to collaborate, in order to comply with the prescribed measures, without prejudice to the responsibility of each of the employers to his/her workers.[72]

63. *Surveillance of workers' health in relation to work.* Subject to any conditions determined by the Commissioner, every employer shall provide for the supervision of the health of the workers exposed to or liable to be exposed to occupational hazards due to pollution and other harmful agents in a working environment.[73]

64. *Duty to provide personal protective equipment.* Employers have a duty to provide and maintain protective equipment for the use of the persons employed.[74]

69. Section 37 Occupational Safety and Health Act, 2006.
70. Section 13, Occupational Safety and Health Act, 2006.
71. Section 23, Occupational Safety and Health Act, 2006.
72. Section 23(2) Occupational Safety and Health Act, 2006.
73. Section 21, Occupational Safety and Health Act, 2006.
74. Section 91(1), Occupational Safety and Health Act, 2006.

65. Duty to ensure the usage of personal protective equipment. An employer shall provide and maintain personal protective equipment, free of charge to employees, and provide instructions for their use.[75]

§5. Relationship Between Ordinary Justice and Sports Justice

66. The term 'justice' simply means that everyone should be treated fairly. The Black's Law Dictionary defines 'justice' as protecting rights and punishing wrongs using fairness.[76] The Courts of Law in Uganda are empowered to dispense justice be it in ordinary justice or sports justice. Depending on the value of the claim sought, claims for ordinary justice or sports justice can be entertained in the Chief Magistrates Courts or the High Court of Uganda. Justice can be sought either in the Civil Courts – which adjudicate disputes between individuals or in criminal courts, which entertain crimes against the State.

67. For civil justice, matters whose monetary claim does not exceed UGX 50,000,000 or the equivalent of USD 14,000, the Chief Magistrates Courts of Uganda can entertain, hear and dispose of.[77] The High Court of Uganda can only entertain the matters whose monetary value exceeds the said amount.[78] These principles apply to both the ordinary and sports justice.

68. For Criminal Justice, a Magistrate Grade One Court can only entertain cases that relate to offences whose maximum penalty is **not** death or life imprisonment. A Chief Magistrates Court may pass any sentence authorized by law except the death sentence.[79] The High Court however can entertain any offence and pass any sentence authorized by law.[80]

69. The Courts of Law in Uganda have handled a number of cases on sports justice. For instance, in *National Council of Sports v. Peter Grace Sseruwagi,*[81] wherein the High Court entertained a claim for compensation by Peter who was on 21 December 1967 appointed as a full-time coach with the National Council of Sports and reported to the National Council of Sports an injury on his back while in the USA on 5 July 1984 during the Olympic games. The court observed that since the accident arose on 5 July 1984, nineteen years had since elapsed and that therefore his suit was time-barred. The court emphasized, in delivering justice, that the public policy behind the statute of limitation has been clear since 1603. A time must

75. Section 91(2), Occupational Safety and Health Act, 2006.
76. Black's Law Dictionary, 2nd Edition.
77. Section 207, Magistrates Courts Act, CAP. 16.
78. Section 14, Judicature Act, CAP. 13.
79. Section 161, Magistrates Courts Act, CAP. 16.
80. Section 14, Judicature Act, CAP. 13.
81. High Court Miscellaneous Application No 305 of 2003.

come when the defendants can relax and know that actions against them are time-barred. It was noted that limitation was an act of peace since long-dormant claims have often more cruelty than justice in them.[82]

70. Another case in point is the one of *Legal Brains Trust Ltd v. Attorney General & Anor.*[83] The applicant therein sought an order for a temporary injunction restraining the Attorney General of Uganda and the National Council of Sports, their agents, servants, or any person from implementing or enforcing Regulations 3(1), 4(4), 20(1) and 20(2) of the National Council of Sports Regulations S. I. No. 38 of 2014. The applicant in this case argued that Government could not transform private sports associations into public bodies. The applicant contended that doing so is a clear expropriation of property and a clear example of excessiveness of power, which is an illegal, irrational and unconstitutional purpose, sought to be achieved. The court went ahead to grant the injunction.

82. *Ibid.*
83. Miscellaneous Application No.638 Of 2014 [2014] UGHCCD.

Part II. Private Sports Organizations and Their Regulations

§1. National Olympic Committee

71. The Uganda Olympic Committee (UOC) was constituted in 1950 and recognized by the IOC in 1956.[84] The UOC represents Uganda in the international sports events like the Olympics (winter and summer) and the Common Wealth Games and among the leading and most noticeable sports occasions in the world that attract the world's best athletes who compete before millions of spectators and sports fans watching them live and on television.

72. The Uganda Olympic Committee is therefore affiliated to: the IOC, the Association of National Olympic Committee, the Common Wealth Games Federation, the Association of National Olympic Committee of Africa and the Islamic Solidarity Sports Federation.

73. In fulfilment of its mandate, the Uganda Olympic Committee is guided by its Constitution, Charter, 2020 Agenda, Quadrennial Plan 2013–2016 and its Strategic Plan. The key strategic objectives guiding the programming and implementation of the Uganda Olympic Committee programmes and whose results and effects, highlighted are: Strategic Objective 1: Governance, Strategic Objective 2: Athlete Development, Strategic Objective 3: Capacity Building, Strategic Objective 4: Organizational Sustainability, Strategic Objective 5: Promoting Olympic Values, Strategic Objective 6: Hosting International Sporting Events.

74. The Uganda Olympic Committee has a mission to act as an agent of the IOC and Common Wealth Games Federation in Uganda to uphold and promote Olympic and Commonwealth ideals to its affiliates and stakeholders by providing support, guiding policy and delivering programmes through its organs and structures.[85] Its vision is to be the best sports governing body in Africa by championing excellence in governance, service delivery, sustainability and sports performance by 2024.[86]

84. Uganda Olympic Committee | Commonwealth Games Association Uganda. Available at http://nocuganda.org/about-us/ (Accessed 15 Jan. 2022).
85. *Ibid.*
86. *Ibid.*

I. Statutes

A. *The Olympic Charter*

75. The Olympic Charter is a set of rules and guidelines for the Organization of the Olympic Games and for governing the Olympic movement. Its last revision was on 17 July 2020 during the 136th IOC Session, held by video conference. Adopted by the IOC, it is the codification of the fundamental principles, rules and bye-laws.

76. The Olympic Charter highlights the mission of the National Olympic Committees (NOCs). It points out that their mission is to develop, promote and protect the Olympic Movement in their respective countries. The role of the National Olympic Committees within each country is to promote the spirit of Olympicism, ensure the observance of the Olympic Charter, and to encourage ethics in and development of sports. They are in charge of their country's representation at the Games, deciding on a host city for the Games, and cooperation with governmental and non-governmental bodies during the Games.[87]

B. *Uganda Olympic Committee Constitution*

77. The Constitution provides that in order to stand for the posts of President, Vice President, Secretary General or Assistant Secretary General, the candidate must be at least 35 years of age and not over 70 years, holder of the minimum of a bachelor's degree from a recognizable institution, and a holder of a diploma in sports from a recognizable institution where the candidate has a sports degree, possesses demonstrable knowledge and experience in leadership, organizational competence and good standing of the Olympic movement and sports in general, a person of integrity and should not have been convicted of an offence involving moral turpitude and must have financial integrity and not be an undischarged bankrupt.

II. Main Regulations

A. *Olympic Movement Code on the Prevention of the Manipulation of Competitions*

78. National Olympic Committees are expected to adopt the Olympic Movement Code on the Prevention of Manipulation of Competitions (OM Code PMC) and to assist their National Sports Federations to develop relevant rules in line with the OM Code PMC, as in national competitions the jurisdiction to investigate and sanction relevant breaches lies with the National Sports Federations.[88]

---

87. Article 28, Olympic Charter.
88. https://olympics.com/ioc/prevention-competition-manipulation/regulations-legislation.

79. In line with Rule 29 of the Olympic Charter, in order to be recognized as a member by the respective NOCs, National Sports Federations should comply with all rules of their respective IF, including this Code.[89]

§2. Major National Federations

80. The different sports disciplines in Uganda have Federations and Associations that govern their respective activities.

I. Federation of Uganda Football Associations

81. The Federation of Uganda Football Associations is the governing body of Association of the Football in Uganda. The association was founded in 1924, and it became affiliated with FIFA in 1960 and the Confederation of African Football in 1961. In 1973, FUFA went ahead and got affiliated with the Council for East and Central Africa Football Associations (CECAFA). CECAFA is an association of the football-playing nations in mostly East Africa and a bit of Central Africa. An affiliate of the Confederation of African Football, CECAFA is the oldest sub-regional football organization on the continent.[90]

II. Uganda Archery Federation

82. In Uganda, the sport of archery was introduced by the late Onegi P'Minga. Uganda Archery Federation is the body registered with National Council of Sports to promote the sport of archery in Uganda and is affiliated to the international body, World Archery Federation in Switzerland. Archery is the practice or skill of using a bow to shoot arrows. It involves the use of a stringed bow to propel arrows towards a target. The object is to shoot your arrows as close to the centre of the target as possible.[91]

83. There are many forms of archery although target archery is the most popular and Olympic recognizable form in Uganda. Others include para archery, field archery, 3D archery, flight and clout archery, ski and run archery.[92]

84. Archery requires that athletes may not raise the bow arm until the signal to start is given. An arrow cannot be re-shot under any circumstances. The arrow may be considered not to have been shot if it falls from the bow or misfires, or if the

89. Rule 29, Olympic Charter.
90. CECAFA. http://www.cecafafootball.org/.
91. Uganda Archery Federation. Available at: https://www.ncs.go.ug/associations/uganda-archery-federation-uaf Accessed 6 Jul. 2021.
92. National Council of Sports. Available at: https://www.ncs.go.ug/associations/uganda-archery-federation-uaf#:~:text=In%20Uganda%2C%20the%20sport%20of,World%20Archery%20Federation%20in%20Switzerland.

target blows or falls over. An arrow that rebounds or hangs from the target will still score based on the mark it makes on the target face. Athletes can be disqualified, have points deducted or be banned from competition for various breaches of rules, based on the severity of the offence. If equipment is damaged, appeals can be made to the judge for such equipment to be replaced or fixed, and any time allowances will be at the judge's discretion. To score, you add up the number of points based on where your arrows hit the target. The highest score for a single arrow is ten for hitting the inner gold ring, while the least (for hitting the outer white ring) is one point. The maximum time permitted to shoot an end of three arrows is two minutes, and four minutes for an end of six arrows.

85. The equipment used includes a bow, arrow, riser and two flexible limbs each ending in a tip with a string nock. Finger protection (including tape or gloves) may be used, as are chest protectors, arm guards for safety and protection.

86. In Uganda, the Uganda Archery Federation is the body registered with the National Council of Sports to promote the sport of archery in Uganda and is affiliated to the international body, the World Archery Federation in Switzerland.[93]

III. The Uganda Swimming Federation

87. The USF is recognized as the only national amateur aquatics sports association responsible for aquatics sports in Uganda, i.e., swimming, open water swimming, diving, water polo, synchronized swimming and master's programme or activities and is affiliated to National Council of Sports (NCS), FINA – Federation Internationale de Natation, CANA – Confederation Africanise de Natation, and UOC – the Uganda Olympic Committee. The Uganda Swimming Federation started in 1978 as an amateur sports association, then called Uganda Swimming Association. The Federation has metamorphosed into what it is currently, a focused and forward-looking organization with plans to overhaul swimming and other water sports. The mission of the Uganda Swimming Federation is to promote and develop swimming and other aquatic sports in Uganda to internationally competitive standards.[94] The Uganda Swimming Federation is responsible for para swimming which is a sport for athletes with different kinds of impairments. The Para Swimming World Series is a top-level international swimming competition for elite para swimmers.[95]

93. Uganda Archery Foundation. https://www.ncs.go.ug/associations/uganda-archery-federation-uaf.
94. Uganda Swimming Federation http://www.ugandaswimming.org/about#about_usf Accessed 4 Jul. 2021.
95. Uganda Paralympic Committee Event Report Singapore 2019 World Para Swimming World Series 31 May 2019. Available at: https://res.cloudinary.com/theugandaswimmingfederation/image/upload/v1560162039/theugandaswimmingfederation/jbotgbdto5ednwob6a0t.pdf (Accessed 2 Feb. 2022).

IV. Uganda Sport Climbing Association

88. The Uganda Sport Climbing Association is responsible for the Sport of Climbing in Uganda and is recognized by the Uganda National Council of Sports. Climbing came to Uganda with the British who ruled it as a protectorate until 1962. The first climbing guide was published in that year. A supplement to the first guide was published in 1963. In 1991, an updated climbing guide was reprinted but contained very few new routes/crags. Uganda has arguably the best mountains in Africa. Tanzania claims the highest mountain (Kilimanjaro) and Kenya (Mt. Kenya), but Uganda has huge mountains that are unspoiled, unique, remote, and see far fewer visitors. The incredible Rwenzori (third highest in Africa) are a true mountain range that soar over 5,100 m and contain glaciers on the equator. The Virunga Mountains in the southwest have pristine trails, gorgeous jungles, rare mountain gorillas, and postcard-quality bamboo zones. The peaks of Moroto, Kadam, Rom, Zulia, Napak and Morungole in Karamoja are almost completely unknown to the outside world and choke full of 'raw' Uganda.

V. Association of Uganda University Sports

89. The Association of Uganda University Sports is responsible for University Sports in Uganda where academic and sports excellence blend. With the vision to live what others dream AUUS spearheads sports of all sorts in institutions of higher learning in Uganda. The AUUS, formerly the National University Sports Federation of Uganda (NUSFU), was formed in 1992 by four higher institutions of learning, namely Makerere, Mbarara University of Science and Technology, Institute of Teacher Education Kyambogo, Islamic University in Uganda. For its years of existence AUUS has organized a number of inter-university games hosted by member institutions including: Makerere University, Kyambogo University, Mbarara University of Science & Technology, Islamic University in Uganda, Ndejje University, Nkumba University, and Uganda Christian University.

VI. Uganda Draughts Association

90. The UDA is responsible for the sport of draughts in Uganda. It aims at promoting interests in the game of draughts and raising the standard of play of the game among the people (youth) in Uganda. It additionally seeks to foster and promote unity among people (youth) through organized competition at district and national levels as well as to promote the game of draughts at national, regional and international levels. The Uganda Draughts Association similarly organizes and manages draughts national competition in Uganda and engages in any such other activity as will enhance the game of draughts.

VII. Uganda Baseball and Softball Association

91. Uganda Baseball and Softball Association (UBASA) is the official governing body for baseball and softball in Uganda. Uganda Baseball and Softball Association works to promote the game of baseball and softball in Uganda. UBASA is responsible for the administration of baseball leagues of all age groups and the training of players, coaches and umpires. They have also instituted development programmes, have worked with partners to both import and purchase equipment for our teams. The association seeks to promote and develop the sport, take the game to all parts of Uganda, engage in national and international competitions, train players, coaches and umpires, ensure the continued growth of the game and use the game of baseball to teach leadership and teamwork.

VIII. Uganda Lacrosse Association

92. The ULA is the legally registered, government licensed, and only World Lacrosse recognized national governing body for the sport of lacrosse in Uganda. ULA believes in the passion, intensity, joy, confidence, and sense of community that lacrosse brings to those who play, coach, and love the sport. From practice to playoffs, we work to make the game better and safer in our nation, ensuring that nothing stands in the way of a player's excitement for the sport. ULA evolves and grows the sport through innovative standards and best practices to advance coach and player development, participation and safety within the fun of the game and its inherent values. As the sport's national governing body and member of the World Lacrosse, the global governing body, ULA also partners with the national sports authority and is fully recognized by the National Council of Sports. ULA's dedication to lacrosse pushes ULA to provide the best certifications, resources and programmes, keeping the spirit and integrity of the game alive for the thousands of athletes who enjoy the fun and benefit of playing. The ULA aims to advance, unify and grow the sport of lacrosse in Uganda with a vision to unite the lacrosse community, promote the game's inherent values, and evolve the sport through innovative standards and programming.

IX. Uganda Volleyball Federation

93. Uganda Volleyball Federation is the supreme governing body of volleyball in Uganda. The Uganda Volleyball Association is a non-profit making association of premier clubs, districts, associations, schools and institutions serving the Ugandan Sportive Community for the development of volleyball in Uganda.[96] The UVF

96. Uganda Volleyball Federation. Available at: https://ugandavolleyballfederation.com.

is a supportive organ of the International Volleyball Federation (FIVB). It recognizes FIVB as the supreme volleyball authority in the world. Henceforth, it is committed to respect and enforce the FIVB Constitution, decisions, rules, regulations and code of conduct.[97]

94. The Mission of UVF is to govern and manage in Uganda all forms of volleyball (including beach volleyball and park volleyball) through professional planning and world-class organization, marketing and promotional activities. It aims to develop as a major entertainment sport in the country. In accordance with the supreme authority in volleyball, UVF works hand in hand with the National Council of Sports, Uganda Olympic Committee and all other sport bodies in Uganda and the rest of the world for the development of sports.[98]

X. Uganda Badminton Association

95. Uganda Badminton Association was formed in the 1960s. The expatriate community, mostly by clubs and schools around Kampala and Jinja, mainly played badminton as a game. The headquarters are in Kampala. Uganda has been a dominant force since 1980 to date in East and Central Africa. In January 2007, in the All Africa Games in Algiers (Algeria), badminton was the first sport to earn Uganda as a country its first medal, a bronze won by Edwin Ekiring. In the 2008 Beijing Olympic Games, Uganda Badminton Association managed to qualify an athlete for the first time in Olympic history. The political turmoil in the country during the 1970s negatively affected the game; however, the sport was rejuvenated in the mid-1980s and a number of clubs were established and started playing the game. Since then, the game has steadily grown taking root in schools very well. Today the game has grown from a few schools and clubs to over eighty schools, twenty higher institutions of learning and ten clubs. It caters for all age groups, right from 4 years to over 70 years and for both men and women. The association has appointed Regional Development Officers across different regions of Uganda in a move to establish the sport nationwide. The Uganda Badminton Association is governed by an Executive Committee of nine people and a patron and is a member of the World Badminton Federation (BWF).

XI. Uganda Cricket Association

96. The UCA seeks to promote interest in the game of cricket and to raise the standard of the game in all communities in Uganda. The Uganda Cricket Association also undertakes to organize and manage cricket matches in Uganda, promote, manage and finance cricket tours in Uganda and abroad and select cricket teams to represent the association both at home and abroad. The Uganda Cricket Association is further responsible for encouraging, supporting and aiding in the establishment of

97. *Ibid.*
98. *Ibid.*

cricket clubs. It seeks to encourage, support and promote umpiring, exercise and take disciplinary action over the members of the association as necessary and arrange, establish, finance and support any scheme for the coaching of players of cricket whether at schools, clubs or elsewhere. The Uganda Cricket Association purposes to acquire by purchase, lease or otherwise and dispose of any such property movable and immovable or any interest therein. In the same vein, the Uganda Cricket Association seeks to manage, layout, prepare and maintain the assets for cricket or other athletic sports and to build or otherwise provide buildings in connection therewith and to furnish, alter, enlarge, repair, uphold and maintain the same. For the same reason, the Uganda Cricket Association seeks to permit such land and buildings to be used by members of the association and others gratuitously or for payment and to dispose of any property in the interest of the association.[99]

XII. The Federation of Motorsport Clubs of Uganda

97. The FMU is a non-profit body controlling all motorsport activities in Uganda. FMU is affiliated to the FIA, which controls all motorsports globally.[100]

XIII. Uganda Boxing Federation

98. Uganda Boxing Federation is the national governing body for boxing. It is responsible for the governance, development and administration of boxing in clubs and competitions. It also represents Uganda as a member of the International Boxing Association (AIBA). As a national governing body, Uganda Boxing Federation is responsible for all the administration, development and promotion of the sport of boxing. It is an association whose founding membership is over sixty clubs forming the federation and is thus overseen by a board of trustees as required by the National Council of Sports. Uganda Boxing Federation is an affiliate member of the NCS, Uganda Olympic Committee (UOC), the African Boxing Confederation (AFBC) and the AIBA. Uganda Boxing Federation is guided by the following core values: accountability – to account for all decisions, actions, and activities of the federation; governance – to provide a strong administration with exemplary and engaging all stakeholders; teamwork – having one boxing family inside and outside the ring; transparency – bring everyone together and accepting positive criticism from everyone irrespective of social, political, economic and cultural attributes; excellence – they strive to excel in all aspects of the sport; and inclusion – working together with

99. Uganda Cricket Association Available at: http://www.ugandacricket.com/index.php/governance/constitution. Accessed 4 Jul. 2021.

100. The Federation of Motorsport Clubs of Uganda – FMU, http://motorsportuganda.com/ Accessed 4 Jul. 2021.

all affiliates and partners locally and internationally. Pillars of Uganda Boxing Federation include technical development, marketing and branding, corporate governance and administration, infrastructure, competitions and membership and fan base.[101]

XIV. VX Uganda

99. The sport of VX was introduced in Uganda in 2006. VX Uganda is the body registered with the National Council of Sport with the mandate to promote the sport of VX in Uganda. Internationally, VX Uganda is affiliated to the Global VX in the United Kingdom. VX Sport (originally Rock-It-Ball) is an indoor ball sport played by two teams of five players on a court that is roughly the size of a sports hall with four badminton courts, basketball courts or squash courts can be used.[102]

XV. The Federation of Uganda Basketball Associations

100. FUBA, the Federation of Uganda Basketball Associations, is the National governing body for basketball in Uganda. Affiliated to NCS and Uganda Olympic Committee (UOC), founded in 1962, they bring together sixty-one basketball teams mainly from the central region of the country and our aim is to spread the game of basketball all over the country. We organize and oversee all national league games, secondary school games, university games, 3X3 Basketball, international competitions that include the zonal qualifiers and club championships when we are hosts. We establish our official basketball rules as well as the regulations that govern the relationships between the different members of the basketball community guided by the FIBA Basketball Rules and Regulations.[103]

XVI. The Uganda Zurkhaneh Sports Association

101. The Uganda Zurkhaneh Sports Association is a Martial Arts Association, which governs different styles martial arts in Uganda. The Uganda Zurkhaneh Sports Association's aim is to teach and promote different martial art styles.[104]

XVII. Uganda Rugby Union

102. The URU is the governing body for rugby in Uganda. It is a national body responsible for the management and development of the sport of rugby in Uganda.

101. Uganda Boxing Federation https://www.ugandaboxingfederation.org/#about Accessed 4 Jul. 2021.
102. VX Uganda https://www.ncs.go.ug/associations/vx-uganda Accessed 4 Jul. 2021.
103. The Federation of Uganda Basketball Associations. Available at: https://fuba.basketball/ Accessed 4 Jul. 2021.
104. The Uganda Zurkhaneh Sports Association. Available at: https://smoothcomp.com/en/club/19576. Accessed 4 Jul. 2021.

The Uganda Rugby Union was established in 1959, and it is responsible for organizing local competitions and responsible for the Rugby Cranes national representative team. The Uganda Rugby Union is a full member of NCS, UOC, Rugby Africa and World Rugby.[105]

XVIII. Uganda Floorball Association

103. UFA is the national governing body for grassroots floorball in the country. Floorball is a type of floor hockey with five field players and a goalkeeper on each side. It is played on a rink, and unlike floor hockey, the floorball stick is relatively short and round in shape. In 2016, the International Floorball Federation (IFF) officially recognized Uganda's Association of the UFA as one of its member countries. The Uganda Floorball Association was founded in 2015 following the numerous strides the game had taken in Uganda. Uganda was the 63rd country to join the International Floorball Federation central board and only Africa's 6th.[106]

XIX. Uganda Handball Federation

104. Uganda Handball Federation is the body mandated to promote the sport of handball in Uganda and is registered with the National Council of Sports and internationally affiliated to the International Handball Federation (IHF) in Switzerland.[107] Handball is a team sport in which two teams of seven players each pass a ball using their hands with the aim of throwing it into the goal of the other team. The object of handball is to score more points than your opponent. Handball is commonly played indoors, but there are other variations such as field handball and beach handball that are played outdoors. Both men and women play handball.

XX. The Uganda Chess Federation

105. The UCF is the governing body of chess competition in Uganda and a member of FIDE, the international chess federation. It administers the official national chess rating system, which awards both numeric ratings and titles of distinction. The UCF is the official umbrella organization for Ugandan chess players and chess supporters of all ages and strengths. The Uganda Chess Federation is affiliated to the World Chess Federation (FIDE), linking Ugandan chess players to

---

105. Uganda Rugby Union https://www.ugandarugby.com/category/press-release/ Accessed 4 Jul. 2021.
106. Uganda Floorball Association gets global recognition, 25 Mar. 2016. Available at: https://kawowo.com/2016/03/25/uganda-floorball-association-gets-global-recognition/ Accessed on 4 Jul. 2021.
107. Uganda Handball Federation https://www.ncs.go.ug/associations/uganda-handball-federation-uhf. Accessed 4 Jul. 2021.

chess players around the world. Uganda participates in international chess competitions like the World Chess Olympiad and other continental events.[108]

XXI. Uganda Rowing Federation

106. URF is the body mandated to promote the sport of rowing in Uganda and is registered with National Council of Sports. Internationally, URF is affiliated to the FISA, the World Rowing Federation in Switzerland. Rowing involves the propelling of a boat using a fixed oar as a lever. The objective of rowing is for the boat that reaches the finish line first to be declared the winner of the race. Reaching the finish line in the quickest possible time requires an astonishing amount of physical and mental strength, high levels of stamina and seamless synchronization when competing in team events.[109]

XXII. Uganda Hockey Federation

107. Uganda Hockey Federation is the body mandated to promote the sport of Hockey in Uganda and is registered with National Council of Sports and is affiliated internationally to the International Hockey Federation in Switzerland. Field hockey is a team sport played on grass, watered turf, artificial turf or synthetic field, as well as an indoor boarded surface. The object of hockey is to hit a ball with a stick into a goal. Every time the ball goes into the goal, then a point is awarded to that team. The team with the most goals at the end of the game is awarded the winner. Each team is made up of eleven players and six substitutes. The hockey players can only hit the ball with the flat side of their stick. Hockey players (other than the goalkeeper) are not allowed to use their feet or any other parts of the body to control the ball at any time. A goal can only be scored from a field goal, a penalty corner, or from a penalty stroke, and hockey players may not trip, push, charge, interfere with, or physically handle an opponent in any way.

XXIII. Uganda Athletics Federation

108. Uganda Athletics Federation is the national governing body of the sports of athletics under the rules and regulations of the IAAF. It is a voluntary, non-profit making body with the mandate of developing and promoting athletics in Uganda in line with the International Association of Athletics Federation Statutes. The federation is managed by volunteers from different education background and all sorts of work. Currently, the Federation is voluntarily managed by professors, lecturers and

---

108. World Trade Directory https://www.worldtradersdirectory.com/listing/uganda-chess-federation-ucf/ Accessed 4 Jul. 2021.
109. Uganda Rowing Federation. Available at: https://www.ncs.go.ug/associations/uganda-rowing-federation-urf Accessed 6 Jul. 2021.

tutors from Kyambogo and Makerere Universities, public servants from the Ministry of Education, Ministry of Gender Labour and Social Development, Ministry of Internal Affairs (Uganda Police & Prison Service), UPDF and individual/private businessmen and women who were time athletes. The Federation's vision is to make athletics the number one sport in Uganda. Its mission is to create a conducive and sustainable environment for talent identification and development in athletics. The Uganda Athletics Federation has the mandate to develop, promote and control sports of athletics within Uganda in accordance with the IAAF rules and regulations. The UAF and its member associations jointly implement athletics activities in the country and prepare athletes for all international competitions held under rules and regulations of global athletics body, IAAF. The Federation collaborates directly with the Ministry of Sports and Education or through the NCS on general development of sports and athletics in schools. It also collaborated with Uganda Olympic Committee (UOC) pertaining to athletics as a key sport of the Olympic movement.[110]

XXIV. Uganda Netball Federation

109. Uganda Netball Federation is the body mandated to promote the sport of netball in Uganda and is fully registered with the National Council of Sports and internationally affiliated to the International Netball Federation (INF) in England. Netball was founded in England and was derived from an early version of basketball. Netball involves two teams where each strives to keep or gain possession of the ball and can be played by both men and women. The team with the ball, through running, jumping, throwing and catching, attempts to move the ball into its goal circle from where a goal may be scored, while the opposing team uses defensive movements and strategies to prevent this and to gain possession.[111]

XXV. Pool Association of Uganda

110. PAU is a sports body mandated by the National Council of Sports to regulate and promote the sport of pool in Uganda. Pool Association of Uganda affiliates to the All Africa Pool Association (AAPA) under the World Pool-Billiard Association (WPA) but also maintains close ties with several other similar sporting bodies in the world. PAU has a fully functional office with an administrative structure, subscribed membership, periodic meetings and assemblies. Overall management is vested in the Executive Committee with specialized functions delegated to Working Committees that have a non-executive majority. The Pool Association of Uganda's mandate and roadmap are detailed in its Constitution and Handbook, the official instruments of reference. The Pool Association of Uganda's mandate includes organizing players into competing teams, training players and umpires, interpreting

110. Uganda Athletes Federation. Available at: https://www.athleticsuganda.org/about.php Accessed 6 Jul. 2021.

111. Uganda Netball Federation. Available at: https://www.ncs.go.ug/associations/uganda-netball-federation-unf Accessed 6 Jul. 2021.

game rules, and participating in local and international competitions. Like all national sports associations, PAU is committed to full compliance with government policy and is currently implementing its master plan by putting emphasis on the following: ensuring national spread through participation of all regions; ensuring a committed and accountable leadership; ensuring the holistic development of players, and brand building in individual players; constantly improving on the image of the sport of pool, and making it marketable; encouraging profile building among players, and exposing them to available opportunities; ensuring game standards through improved game venues and equipment; encouraging skills advancement through player ranking, which stimulates competition; diversifying from blackball to include other codes of pool and disciplines of billiard sports; encouraging the specific participation of ladies at individual and team levels; encouraging the participation of the youth through schools, institutions, and academies; ensuring constitutionalism; and building and maintaining a professional dependable National Pool Team. As part of its strategic plan, Pool Association of Uganda will establish several sports-related incomes generating programmes to sustain its existence and fund its road map. This necessitates the broadening of existing structures to accommodate non-traditional roles, and Pool Association of Uganda has been reincorporated under the Trusteeship Act as a measure in that direction. The Strategic Plan seeks to address the following priority areas: Structural Overhaul – Bringing all regional bodies and Cue sport disciplines together to form a Federation, Infrastructure Development – Focusing on the establishment of games facilities managed by the Federation, Human Resource Development – Focusing on training of Referees, Coaches, and Sports Managers, Marketing & Publicity – Branding and Strategic Positioning thereby encouraging endorsements and Sustainability – Income Generation and Accountable Management.[112]

XXVI. Uganda Ultimate Frisbee Association

111. In Uganda, the sport was introduced around 2006 and was fully registered with National Council of Sports in 2010. Uganda Ultimate Frisbee Association is the body mandated to promote the sport of Ultimate Frisbee in Uganda and is registered with National Council of Sports and internationally affiliated to the World Flying Disc Federation in the USA. Ultimate Frisbee is a non-contact team sport played with a flying disc (Frisbee). On a field of play, each team comprises seven players and can be played by both men and women. The objective of the game is to score points by passing the disc into the opposing end zone, similar to American Football and Rugby. The winner is usually decided by whichever team is first to score a specified number of goals or whichever team scores the most goals in a given time frame.[113]

---

112. Uganda Pool Association. Available at: https://poolug.org/profile/ Accessed 6 Jul. 2021.
113. Uganda Ultimate Frisbee Association. Available at: https://www.ncs.go.ug/associations/uganda-ultimate-frisbee-association-uufa Accessed 6 Jul. 2021.

XXVII. Uganda Fencing Association

112. Fencing was founded in Uganda in 2006 and UFA is the body mandated to promote the sport of Fencing in Uganda and is registered with National Council of Sports. Fencing is a combat sport in which two competitors fight using 'rapier-style' swords. The object of fencing is to use your weapon to strike your opponent while avoiding being hit yourself. The sport is simple, ruthless and – if you get it wrong, painful. Competitive fencing takes on three varieties: foil, sabre and epée.[114]

XXVIII. Uganda Cycling Association

113. Uganda Cycling Association unites all Cyclists in Uganda being the governing body in the country. Its main objective is to develop and promote all aspects of cycling in Uganda. This is because cycling is more than just a competitive sport. It is also a leisure activity and an environmentally friendly means of transport nationally and internationally.

XXIX. The Kabaddi Federation of Uganda

114. The KFU is the central body for the administration and promotion of game of Kabaddi in Uganda. Established in 2017, KFU is preceded by the International Kabaddi Federation, which came into existence in 1950. The federation has organized international Kabaddi tournaments for both men and women, in Uganda. Sub-junior and junior nationals and zonal competitions are also held by KFU, to promote the game at the local level. Kabaddi is a contact sport that originated in Ancient India. The game of Kabaddi shall be governed and played under the following rules and regulations of International Kabaddi Federation (IKF).[115]

XXX. American Football Association of Uganda

115. American Football Association of Uganda is the body mandated to promote the sport of American Football in Uganda. In 2019, the association got formal registration with National Council of Sports and is affiliated internationally to the International Federation of American Football in France. American Football is a team sport played by two teams of eleven players on a rectangular field with goal-posts at each end. The object of American Football is to score more points than your opponents in the allotted time. To do this they must move the ball down the pitch

114. Uganda Fencing Association Available at: https://www.ncs.go.ug/associations/uganda-fencing-association-ufa Accessed 6 Jul. 2021.
115. The Kabaddi Federation of Uganda (KFU). Available at: https://www.kabaddifu.co.ug/ Accessed 6 Jul. 2021.

in phases of play before eventually getting the ball into the 'end zone' for a touchdown. This can be achieved by either throwing the ball to a teammate or running with the ball.[116]

XXXI. Uganda Golf Union

116. Uganda Golf Union is the body mandated to promote the sport of pool in Uganda and is registered with National Council of Sports and internationally affiliated to the International Golf Federation in Switzerland. Golf is a game played in an open field or 'teeing ground' in which a ball is struck with a club. The object is to get your ball from the tee (the starting point of any hole) to the green and ultimately into the hole in as few shots as possible.[117]

XXXII. Uganda Taekwondo Federation

117. Uganda Taekwondo Association was founded in the early 70s, and by 1973, its Chairperson and former Commissioner of Uganda Prisons, Mr. Etima, was elected to the World Taekwondo Federation Executive Committee. Uganda Taekwondo Association became a Federation in 2004, given the growing number of affiliate clubs and desire to adopt international standards of sports management. Uganda Taekwondo Federation (UTF) is affiliated to the World Taekwondo Federation (WTF), with headquarters in Seoul, South Korea, and to the Africa Taekwondo Union (AFTU), whose seat is in Cairo, Egypt. All Taekwondo competitions, junior and senior, organized or sanctioned by the Uganda Taekwondo Federation in Uganda, are governed in accordance with World Taekwondo Federation rules and regulations. Our Vision is nurturing a fit, healthy and sane society through commitment to the practice of Taekwondo. Our Mission is promoting Taekwondo in Uganda as sport and lifestyle by opening up 'do jangs' (Taekwondo gyms) and encouraging massive participation countrywide. Uganda Taekwondo Federation is led by an Executive Committee, elected for a four-year term of office, in line with the Olympic movement requirements, with a President, Vice President, Secretary General, Assistant Secretary General, Treasurer and Organising Secretary. These officials are assisted by a five other Committee Members who take charge of the Technical, Medical, Disciplinary and Organising Sub-Committees. Uganda Taekwondo Federation is made up of affiliate Taekwondo clubs based in different major towns of Uganda, such as Kampala, Gulu, Arua, Jinja, Lira and Tororo. Member clubs pay affiliation fees and take part in an annual national league and several open competitions under Uganda Taekwondo Federation patronage. Star athletes from the

116. American Football Association of Uganda. Available at: https://www.ncs.go.ug/associations/american-football-association-uganda-afau (Accessed 6 Jul. 2021).
117. Uganda Golf Union Available at: https://www.ncs.go.ug/associations/uganda-golf-union-ugu Accessed 6 Jul. 2021.

various clubs are given an opportunity to represent Uganda in regional and international championships. The affiliate clubs also benefit from quality technical guidance dispensed by World Taekwondo Federation-approved coaches and referees, as well as the distribution of special Taekwondo sports equipment.[118]

XXXIII. Uganda Squash Rackets Association

118. Uganda Squash Rackets Association is the body mandated to promote the sport of Squash in Uganda and is registered with National Council of Sports and is affiliated internationally to World Squash Federation in UK. Squash is a racket and ball sport played by two players on a four-walled indoor enclosed court with a small, hallow rubber ball. The object of the game is to hit the ball off the back wall until you manage to make your opponent fail in returning the ball. Every time you do so, you will receive a point. Points make up sets, which in turn determine the winner of the match.[119]

XXXIV. Uganda Paralympic Committee

119. Uganda Paralympic Committee (UPC) develops, coordinates and promotes Sports for people with disabilities. We are a National sports body in Uganda and work in all districts to further this cause. Uganda Paralympic Committee works with its different Sports Associations and other stakeholders like Disabled People's Organizations, the government, International Sports Bodies and main stream sports federations. This it ensures the development and activeness of its member Associations and strengthens its partnerships with the stakeholders. This encourages our athletes to aim towards Paralympic Games because it is the high point of all Paralympic athletes, they inspire others and encourage them to join and participate in Paralympic sports.[120]

§3. Statutes

I. National Council of Sports Act, Cap 32 of 1964

120. The *NCS* is a statutory body under the Ministry of Education and Sports that was established by the National Council of sports Act, Cap 32 of 1964. Sports in Uganda is mandated and driven by the Ministry of Education and Sports (MES) which is a cabinet level ministry of Uganda. Ministry of Education and Sports is mandated 'to provide technical support, guide, coordinate, regulate and promote

---

118. Uganda Taekwondo Federation Available at: https://www.ncs.go.ug/associations/uganda-taekwondo-federation-utf (Accessed 7 Jul. 2021).
119. Uganda Squash Rackets Association Available at: https://www.ncs.go.ug/associations/uganda-squash-rackets-association-usra (Accessed 7 Jul. 2021).
120. Uganda Paralympic Committee Available at: https://ugandaparalympic.org/about-us/ (Accessed 7 Jul. 2021).

quality education, training and sports to all persons in Uganda for national integration, development and individual advancement'. Under Ministry of Education and Sports, sports are managed under the Department of Physical Education and Sports. However, other organs through the Ministry Education and sports for example the National Council of Sports and the Uganda Olympic Committee also play an active role in regulating sports activities in Uganda.

121. Under the National Council of Sports Act, Cap 32 of 1964, National Council of Sports is mandated among other functions: to develop and promote all forms of sport on a national basis, in conjunction with voluntary amateur sports bodies; to provide training and the required staff; and to encourage and facilitate cooperation among the various National Sports Associations in Uganda.

122. National Council of Sports develops and promotes all forms of sport on national basis, in conjunction with voluntary amateur sports bodies, and provides training and the required staff. It encourages and facilitates cooperation among the various national sports associations. It approves international and national sports competitions and festivals organized by national and other associations. It organizes, in conjunction with the national associations, national and international competitions and festivals as a means of gaining experience and the Minister may approve fostering friendly relations with other nations, and other activities as: stimulates interest in sports at all levels; plans the general policy of sports promotion; awards, in consultation with the national associations, medals, diplomas, certificates and other incentives for the encouragement and promotion of sporting activities; sponsor scholarships for the training of coaches and organizers; advises the Minister of Sports regarding external relations in the field of sports; arranges with local authorities for the provision of sporting facilities at all local levels and to inculcate a high level of sportsmanship and discipline; approves expenditure of national associations in receipt of grants made or through the Council and to audit the accounts of such associations.

123. The National Council of Sports Act cap 13 mandates the General Secretary to oversee the administration and day-to-day operations of the Council. The General Secretary is responsible for the execution of the policies of the Council and carries out all other such duties as may be assigned by the Council. The General is therefore responsible for the strategic planning, accountability and overall implementation of the Council's mandate.

124. The National Council of Sports which is also linked to the Supreme Council for Sports in Africa and other relevant sports organizations serves as a regulator and apex organization that coordinates all sports activities in the country in conjunction with the registered National Sports Associations/Federations.

II. The Statutes of the Federation of Uganda Football Associations

125. FUFA is a private organization of an associative nature comprised of the following members: the sixteen FUFA 1st Division Clubs; the 2nd Division League; the eight Regional Football Associations; the Uganda Football Players Association; the Uganda Women Football Association; the Uganda Football Coaches Association; the Uganda Football Referees Association; the Uganda Beach-Soccer Association; the Uganda Schools Football Association; the Uganda Youth Football Association and the FUFA Women Elite League.[121] The Association owns a private Trust incorporated under the Trustees Incorporation Act.

126. The statutes enumerate the objectives of the Association to include the following: to improve the game of football constantly and promote, regulate and control it throughout the territory of Uganda in the light of fair play and its unifying, educational, cultural and humanitarian values, particularly through youth and development programmes; to organize competitions in Association Football in all its forms at a national level, by defining precisely, as required, the areas of authority conceded to the various Leagues of which it is composed; to draw up regulations and provisions and ensure their enforcement; to protect the interests of its Members; to respect and prevent any infringement of the statutes, regulations, directives and decisions of FIFA, of CAF and FUFA as well as the Laws of the Game and to ensure that these are also respected by its Members; to promote integrity, ethics and fair play with a view to preventing all methods or practices, such as corruption, doping or match manipulation, which might jeopardize the integrity of matches, competitions, players, officials and members or give rise to abuse of Association Football, futsal or beach soccer; to control and supervise all friendly football matches of all forms played throughout the territory of FUFA; to manage international sporting relations connected with Association Football in all its forms and To host competitions at international and other levels.[122]

127. The statutes also indicate that FUFA and each of its Members shall play Association Football in compliance with the Laws of the Game issued by IFAB. Only IFAB may lay down and alter the Laws of the Game.[123]

128. The statutes also provide that FUFA and each of its Members shall play futsal and beach soccer in accordance with the Futsal Laws of the Game and the Beach Soccer Laws of the Game. Only FIFA may lay down and alter' the Futsal Laws of the Game and the Beach Soccer Laws of the Game.[124]

---

121. Article 10 of the Statutes of the Federation of Uganda Football Associations. Available at: www.fufa.co.ug%2Fwp-content%2Fuploads%2F2020%2F08%2FFUFA-Statutes.pdf&clen=416649&chunk=true.
122. Article 2 of the Statutes of the Federation of Uganda Football Associations.
123. Article 6(1) of the Statutes of the Federation of Uganda Football Associations.
124. Article 6(2) of the Statutes of the Federation of Uganda Football Associations.

129. The statutes also provide for a FUFA Licensing Committee which is mandated to deal with matters of examining, verifying and advising the executive committee about the compliance and capability of FUFA licensees including but not limited to clubs, football competitions, player agents, match agents and academies.[125]

130. The statutes also provide for the establishment of a Legal Committee which is tasked with analysing basic legal issues relating to football and the evolution of the Statutes and Regulations of FUFA and its members.[126]

§4. Main Regulations

I. The National Council of Sports Regulations, 2014

131. These regulations provide for the mandatory incorporation of a National Sports Associations in Uganda.[127] A National Sports Association is defined to mean an organization promoting and supervising a particular sport throughout the country and includes a federation.[128]

132. Every National Sports Association is required to be registered with the National Council of Sports,[129] and the National Council of Sports is forbidden from registering more than one sports association in respect of each sport in Uganda.[130] The registered national association must maintain a register of all persons who are members of the association.[131] Executive management of the National Sports Associations is reserved for Ugandan citizens who have participated in the sport or been involved in the administration of the sport.[132]

133. The National Council of Sports is mandated with the responsibility to issue a certificate of recognition to every national sports association it recognizes.[133] Recognized National Sports Associations are entitled to funding as provided in the Regulations.[134] In this regard, the National Council of Sports is obliged to publish a list of the national sports associations it recognizes at least once every year by notice in the gazette and at least two newspapers of nationwide circulation.[135] Associations that use the word ‘Uganda‘ in reference to entities that are not recognized by the national council of sports commit an offence and the responsible persons are

125. Article 48 of the Statutes of the Federation of Uganda Football Associations.
126. Article 51 of the Statutes of the Federation of Uganda Football Associations.
127. Regulation 3(1) of the National Council of Sports regulations, 2014.
128. Regulation 3(2) of the National Council of Sports regulations, 2014.
129. Regulation 4(1) of the National Council of Sports regulations, 2014.
130. Regulation 4(3) of the National Council of Sports regulations, 2014.
131. Regulation 5(1) of the National Council of Sports regulations, 2014.
132. Regulation 7(1) of the National Council of Sports regulations, 2014.
133. Regulation 9(3) of the National Council of Sports regulations, 2014.
134. Part V of the National Council of Sports regulations, 2014.
135. Regulation 10 of the National Council of Sports regulations, 2014.

liable on conviction to imprisonment not exceeding six months.[136] Every national association has access to sports facilities owned or managed by the National Council of Sports in accordance with a schedule drawn up by the council.[137]

134. The recognition of a National Sports Association may be withdrawn by the National Council of Sports where the international body governing the sport suspends the association or withdraws its recognition from the association; or where the association ceases to meet the requirements of a national sports association.[138] Where the National Council of Sports ceases to recognize a National Sports Association, the council must notify the association in writing and give public notice in the gazette and at least two newspapers with nationwide circulation.[139]

135. The regulations also establish the National Forum of Sports Associations whose core mandate is: to recommend to the Minister responsible for sports the strategies for promoting and developing sports; to attract and solicit funding and partnerships for sports; to advise the Minister on the nature of assistance and support to be given to a national sports association representing Uganda abroad; and to assist the National Council of Sports in branding sports in the country.[140]

II. FUFA Club Licensing Rules 2020/2021

136. The regulations shall establish binding rules and procedure to issuance of a licence to a football club/team to participate in football competitions by setting minimum requirements and procedure to be followed by the licensor and the Licensee.[141]

137. The regulations seek to achieve the following objectives: to set minimum standards in football; to enforce good football governance by safeguarding the credibility and integrity of club competitions; to ensure and enforce clubs' financial stability and transparency; to enhance fans development by clubs; to ensure and enforce sporting values in accordance with the principles of fair play as well as safe and secure match environments; to ensure and enforce commitment to youth education and development; to improve the level of professionalism within the football family; to ensure and enforce transparency in the ownership of clubs; to ensure and enforce transparency in the control of clubs; and to produce professionally prepared players for the national teams; to create and sustain a football economy.[142]

138. Clubs which qualify for the 1st, 2nd and 3rd FUFA Football Divisions and other organized/authorized competitions on sporting merit are required to obtain a

136. Regulation 11(3) of the National Council of Sports regulations, 2014.
137. Regulation 19(1) of the National Council of Sports regulations, 2014.
138. Regulation 12(1) of the National Council of Sports regulations, 2014.
139. Regulation 12(3) of the National Council of Sports regulations, 2014.
140. Regulation 17 of the National Council of Sports regulations, 2014.
141. Regulation 4 of the FUFA Club Licensing Rules 2020/2021.
142. Regulation 3 of the FUFA Club Licensing Rules 2020/2021.

FUFA club licence to participate in the competitions.[143] The licence obtained by these clubs expires without prior notice at the end of the season for which it was issued,[144] and it is forbidden to transfer it.[145]

139. The licence may be withdrawn by the licensor's decision-making bodies in the event that any of the conditions for the issuing of a licence are no longer satisfied, the licensee violates any of its obligations under the FUFA club licensing regulations or the licensee violates FUFA Rules and fails to undertake corrective measures as decided by FUFA.[146]

140. The regulations provide for the First Instance Body decides on whether a licence shall be granted to an applicant on the basis of the documents provided and in accordance with the provisions of these regulations at the submission deadline set by the Licensor. The FUFA Executive Committee decides on the composition of the First Instance Body.[147]

141. The regulations also provide for the Appeals Body which must decide on appeals submitted against the decision of the First Instance Body in writing and make a final and binding decision on whether a licence shall be granted or not. Appeals may only be lodged by the Licence Applicant following a refusal or withdrawal of licence by the First Instance Body.[148]

142. A club may also be licensed through the Extraordinary Application of the Club Licensing System. Under this system, if a club qualifies for a national or international club competition based on its sporting results but has not undergone a national licensing process at all or has undergone a licensing process which is lower/ not equivalent to the one applicable to top-division clubs because it belongs to a division other than the top division, the Licensor may on behalf of such a club – request the extraordinary application of the club licensing system.[149] Based on such an extraordinary application, the relevant body organizing the respective club competition can grant special permission to enter the corresponding club competition which only applies to that specific applicant and for the season in question.[150]

143. The regulations provide for the minimum requirements that the Licensor must put in place for the verification of the criteria described in the FIFA Regulations (sporting criteria, infrastructure criteria, personnel and administrative criteria and legal criteria and financial criteria) in order to control the issue of a licence to a Licence Applicant.[151]

143. Regulation 5(1)(i) of the FUFA Club Licensing Rules 2020/2021.
144. Regulation 5(1)(iii) of the FUFA Club Licensing Rules 2020/2021.
145. Regulation 5(1)(iv) of the FUFA Club Licensing Rules 2020/2021.
146. Regulation 5(1)(v) Regulation 5(1)(iii) of the FUFA Club Licensing Rules 2020/2021.
147. Regulation 8 of the FUFA Club Licensing Rules 2020/2021.
148. Regulation 9 of the FUFA Club Licensing Rules 2020/2021.
149. Regulation 11 of the FUFA Club Licensing Rules 2020/2021.
150. *Ibid.*
151. Regulation 12 of the FUFA Club Licensing Rules 2020/2021.

144. For Professional League Clubs, the requirements for the financial criteria entail the following: the proof of payment to FUFA of the Licence Application Fees as set by FUFA; the Annual Financial Statements for the previous Financial Year of the Club; the club's balanced or surplus budget for the entire season for which the application is made to the licensor; written confirmations by persons of authority from the sources of funds included as income to the club in the budget. This includes letter of guarantee from sponsors that have contracts with the club; the Club Bank Statement for the last 6 months to date of submission; proof from the bank that the club CEO is a principal signatory to the club bank account; and proof of payment of players and coaches every three months.[152]

145. The requirements under the sporting criteria entail the following: the FUFA License for the Football Academy of minimum of Class B owned and operated by the club; contracts of all players registered by the club. Registration of players will be done in accordance with the relevant regulations; pre-competition medical reports for each player in accordance with the medical requirements.[153]

146. When it comes to infrastructure criteria, the following ought to be submitted: the FUFA Stadium Certificate of the minimum of level 3 for the 1st Division and level 4 for the 2nd Division whose date of expiry is after the end of the season for which the application is being made; documents of security of tenure such as: copies of certificate of title in case of freehold, mailo and/or lease tenure ownership, license to occupy and any sub-leases, legally enforceable agreement from the owner for its use by the club, expiring not earlier than the end of the current season relating thereto. This Agreement is submitted with the letter of guarantee of prioritization of the club fixtures ahead of any other event.[154]

III. FUFA Competition Rules 2014

147. These provide for types of football competitions in Uganda. One of the types is a League which is a competition where all participating teams play against each other on a home-away basis over a period of time either in a single format or groupings. Where groupings are established, stage one competition shall involve teams in each group playing on league format over a period of time with playoffs in stage two of the competition.

148. Other competitions include: mini-league which is a competition where all participating teams play against each other over one leg, mixed-format Competition which is a competition where participating teams are drawn into groups and group teams playing against each other on a mini-league basis with topping team(s) per group qualifying for a knock-out stage to determine the competition champion and

---

152. Regulation 14(1) of the FUFA Club Licensing Rules 2020/2021.
153. Regulation 14(2) of the FUFA Club Licensing Rules 2020/2021.
154. *Ibid.*

knock-out competition which is a competition where the winning team of each pair of teams competing qualifies to the next competition.[155]

149. The rules provide for the establishment of several FUFA Committees. The FUFA Licensing Committee is tasked with managing the licences issued by FUFA to clubs, competition organizers, academies, coaches, agents etc. It is mandated to collect and compile the licensee data, evaluate the data and award or not award the licence based on regulations drawn by FUFA. The FUFA Players Status Committee is in charge of the status of players and adjudges on contractual disputes of players with their clubs, their agents and coaches with the employers. The FUFA Referees Standing Committee is responsible for development, appointment and technical discipline of Referees and Match Assessors. The FUFA Safety and Security Committee is in charge of Safety and Security that is mandated to advice on security matters of FUFA Competitions and FUFA Competitions Matches. It may recommend the level of security required for a particular competition or match.

150. The FUFA Disciplinary Committee is a Judicial Body that is mandated to adjudge FUFA Competitions matters of forgery, bribery, doping, match fixing. The FUFA Disciplinary Committee is also mandated to act on FUFA Competitions matters brought before it by any other FUFA organ or upon its own observation of defaulting inclusive of media stories. The FUFA Disciplinary Committee shall also work as an Appeals Body for decisions made by lower judicial units. The FUFA Appeals Committee is a Judicial Body that works as an Appeals Body for the decisions of the FDC or FUFA Players Status.

151. Committee, FRSC and FUFA Licensing Board. The Decision of the FUFA Appeals Committee is final.[156]

152. For representation in International Club Competitions, FUFA reserves the final authority to determine the club to represent Uganda in all international club competitions without compromising sporting integrity.[157]

153. The Rules provide for a FUFA E-License Plus Electronic Registration System and the registration of players and officials of the clubs in 1st to 3rd Division leagues must be done under the FUFA web-based electronic system called FUFA e-License Plus. Each club is accordingly obliged to equip club office with system mandatory equipment including a computer or laptop, printer, scanner and Internet access.[158] The FUFA Competitions matches must be played in accordance with the current FIFA Laws of the game.[159]

155. Article 12 of the FUFA Competitions Rules.
156. Article 6(3) of the FUFA Competitions Rules.
157. Article 16(1) of the of the FUFA Competitions Rules.
158. Article 19(7) & (8) of the FUFA Competitions Rules.
159. Article 24(1) of the FUFA Competitions Rules.

154. The rules also provide a procedure for registering protests, petition, defence, complaints, and appeal.

155. A protest means intent to petition infringement of these regulations that may require evidence of the instance (photographs, audio and video bytes). For an infringement of these rules that require instant evidence for a particular match, such match shall be played under protest and for a match to be played under protest, the protest must be registered with the Match Commissioner, or in his absence, with the Centre Referee before the match kick off. Any protest raised during the match shall be null and void.[160]

156. A Petition means a formal and/or written follow-up of a protest and for a protest to stand, a petition must be filed with the TOC upon payment of the requisite fees and only within forty-eight hours after the match. Any petition logged outside this regulatory period shall be null and void.[161]

157. A complaint shall mean a formal and written infringement of the regulations that may not require evidence of the instance and has no consequence on a result of a match already played. A complaint shall be filed within seven days before or after the incident of rules infringement. Any complaint by a club against a match official shall be forwarded to the FUFA. Depending on the merit of the complaint, the FUFA Competent bodies shall conduct investigations and actions, such a match official (s) may not officiate in any match of respective competition until the matters are concluded.[162]

158. Appeal means a formal and written expression of discontent with a decision of any of the judicial units to a higher judicial unit. All appeals shall be made in writing to the next Judicial Body within forty-eight hours from the date of receipt of the decision of the judicial unit by the concerned party. Such appeal shall be accompanied by a non-refundable fee. Failure to log an appeal within forty-eight hours from the date of receipt of the decision shall mean acceptance of the decision. An appeal to the final appellant body the FUFA Appeals Committee shall be determined within 30 days and its decision shall be final.[163]

159. Any official, coach, player or fan of a club who causes to be published in the media or makes a statement to the media, on a matter of appeal or hearing before any of the judicial units, shall be subjected to disciplinary action by FUFA and the judicial unit may consequently nullify the petition, complain or appeal.[164]

160. Article 30 of the FUFA Competitions Rules.
161. *Ibid.*
162. *Ibid.*
163. *Ibid.*
164. *Ibid.*

IV. The Lotteries and Gaming Act

160. Ugandan gambling laws were updated in 2016 with the creation of the Lotteries and Gaming Act,[165] which established the National Lotteries and Gambling Regulatory Board. The NLGRB issues licenses and oversees all betting activities here. The Lotteries and Gaming Act of 2016 further streamlined Ugandan gambling laws. And the Lotteries and Gaming Act (Amendment) 2017[166] reduced the gaming tax from 35% to 20%.

161. The Lotteries and Gaming Act, 2016 reformed and consolidated legislation on lotteries, gaming, betting and casino activities, and accordingly repealed the National Lotteries Act (Cap. 191) and the Gaming and Pool Betting (Control and Taxation) Act (Cap 292).

162. The Lotteries and Gaming Act, 2016, provides for a Board, operational licenses, minimum capital requirements, increased gaming tax, fit and proper requirements, restrictions on minors and the establishment of a national electronic monitoring system. The National Lotteries and Gaming Regulatory Board is established as an independent body to supervise and regulate the establishment and operation of lottery, gaming, betting and casinos.[167] In addition to regulating lotteries, gaming and betting, the Lotteries and Gaming Act, 2016 contains detailed provisions regulating the establishment and operation of casinos. This includes licensing of the casino premises, casino employees, games and gaming machines and equipment.[168] The Lotteries and Gaming Act, 2016 introduced regulation of Public Lotteries in Uganda and defines them to include any game of chance involving the selection of specific numbers that are tied to winning a prize.[169]

163. The Lotteries and Gaming Act, 2016 provides for fit and proper requirements for persons intending to operate a national lottery. It states that before the Board can recommend to the Minister responsible for Finance to issue a national lottery licence, it must satisfy itself that the applicant is fit and proper to conduct a national lottery.[170] In determining whether a person is fit and proper to do so, the Board shall take into consideration factors like experience, knowledge and character, financial adequacy, public interests and any other matter prescribed by the Minister responsible for Finance.[171]

164. A person licensed to conduct a lottery under the Lotteries and Gaming Act, 2016 is required to ensure that the lottery rules are approved by the Board prior to running the lottery.[172] Such rules are published at least fourteen days before the

165. Came into force on 8 Apr. 2016.
166. Came into force on 13 Jun. 2017.
167. Part II of the Lotteries and Gaming Act, 2016.
168. Part V of the Lotteries and Gaming Act, 2016.
169. Section 1 of the Lotteries and Gaming Act, 2016.
170. Section 23(1) of the Lotteries and Gaming Act, 2016.
171. Section 23(2) of the Lotteries and Gaming Act, 2016.
172. Section 25(1) of the Lotteries and Gaming Act, 2016.

lottery, in a newspaper widely circulated in the area where the lottery is to be conducted.[173] These rules must also be kept or exhibited in a conspicuous place at the licensed premises.[174]

165. The National Lotteries and Gaming Regulatory Board is authorized to issue the following operating licences: a national lottery licence; a public lottery licence; a casino operating licence; a bingo operating licence; a pool betting operating licence; a betting intermediary licence; a gaming or betting machine general operating licence; a licence to manufacture, supply, install, adapt, maintain or repair a gaming or betting machine, or a part of it; and a licence to manufacture, supply, install or adapt gambling software.[175] Two or more licences may also be combined and issued in one licence.[176]

166. The Lotteries and Gaming Act, 2016 requires the registration of gaming and betting machines, and widely defines a gaming or betting machine or device to include any equipment (mechanical, electro-mechanical or electronic), component, machine or software which is used in connection with gaming and betting whether directly or remotely.[177] It further provides that the Minister responsible for finance may, by statutory instrument: require applicants of licences of a specified category or class of a licence to provide a security bond in the nature and amount to be specified by the Minister;[178] prescribe minimum capital requirements for a licence;[179] and determine the standards in respect of the manufacture, supply, installation, adaptation, maintenance or repair of gaming or betting machines and software.

167. The Lotteries and Gaming Act, 2016 prohibits licence holders from accepting payments from minors (persons below 25 years)[180] or allowing minors to access the casino or gaming and betting premises. Licencees and their agents are required to prominently display a notice to that effect. This has been in response to public outcry for protective measures in favour of the youth population. Adults are also prohibited from subscribing to a public lottery on behalf of a minor.[181] The Lotteries and Gaming Act, 2016 mandates the Board to establish and maintain a national central electronic monitoring system.[182] This is aimed at detecting and monitoring any irregular transactions or significant events associated with casino, gaming and betting activity. It is envisaged that every licensee will be required to obtain software that connects them to the central system to enable real time monitoring of transactions and tax computation.

173. Section 25(5) of the Lotteries and Gaming Act, 2016.
174. Section 25(2) of the Lotteries and Gaming Act, 2016.
175. Section 27 of the Lotteries and Gaming Act, 2016.
176. Section 27(5) of the Lotteries and Gaming Act, 2016.
177. Section 1 of the Lotteries and Gaming Act, 2016.
178. Section 40(1) of the Lotteries and Gaming Act, 2016.
179. Section 39 of the Lotteries and Gaming Act, 2016.
180. Section 1 of the Lotteries and Gaming Act, 2016.
181. Part IX of the Lotteries and Gaming Act, 2016.
182. Section 61 of the Lotteries and Gaming Act, 2016.

Part III. Sport and Employment

Introduction

168. Uganda has a variety of career opportunities for persons involved in the sports, health and recreation industry. The sports industry requires knowledge, skills and a good degree of understanding in areas such as sport management and delivery, and in service delivery essential for athlete preparation and specialized fitness industries. There are also opportunities for training in professional service provision and research in programmes such as the Bachelor of Science in Sports Science offered at different universities in Uganda. These programmes enable one to become a Sport and Exercise Scientist.

169. There is a range of choices of varied career paths in the Sports Industry in Uganda with skills which lead to diverse employment opportunities. For instance, several opportunities exist in areas such as Elite Athlete Preparation, Strength and Conditioning, Fitness and General Coaching, Sports Administration and Management. When it comes to conducting research: Graduate training in exercise rehabilitation and sport physiotherapy are available. In teaching: teaching and coaching careers, school – physical education teaching (primary and secondary), non-school settings: coaching – schools, sports clubs, community sport, fitness – and Health-related careers, cardiac rehabilitation (fitness for health), movement rehabilitation (sports physiotherapy), sports and health nutrition, corporate fitness (health and fitness instruction), specific sport fitness coaching, personal trainers, etc. When it comes to sport management careers, the following are available: Athletic/Sports-Federation Administration, District Sports Administration (Local Government), Sport and Leisure Management (Private), Sport Retailing, Resort Sport Management, Facility management, etc. In Sport Media careers, Journalism – News Papers (writing), Radio Presenters, TV Presenters, Sports Photography, Sports Art, etc. furthermore, there are several Sport-Related careers. Sports Law, Performance Analysis, Sport and Exercise Science Research, Sports, Leisure and Hospitality Consultancy, Sports Officiating, Sports Entrepreneur, etc.

§1. Sources of Employment Law

170. Uganda inherited the British common law and is therefore a common law country and since Independence in 1962, attempts are being made to enact laws with domestic cultural values and aspirations. There exists an anachronistic national law governing the regulation and management of sports in Uganda. Among the key labour laws in Uganda are, the Workers Compensation Act 2000, the Minimum Wages Act 2000, the Employment Act 2006, the Labour Union Arbitration and Settlement Act 2006 and the Occupational Safety Act 2006. The Employment Act 2006, outlines the conditions of employment including, contract of service, termination of contract, termination notices, and protection of wages, hours of work, rest and holidays, employment of women, employment of children and care of employees. Likewise, the Workers Compensation Act 2000 entitles employees to automatic compensation for any personal injury from an accident arising out and in the course of his/her employment even if the injury results from the employee's negligence. The Act further details that, for an injury that leads to death, the compensation should be equivalent to an employer's monthly pay multiplied by 60 months.

I. Ordinary Law

171. There are five sources of Employment law in Uganda and these include:

(1) *The Constitution of the Republic of Uganda, 1995.* This is the supreme law of the land and all other laws must conform to it. In the event that any law is inconsistent with the Constitution, the Constitution of the Republic of Uganda, 1995 takes precedence.[183] Article 40 clause 2 of the Constitution of the Republic of Uganda, as amended stipulates that, 'Every person in Uganda has the right to practice his or her profession and to carry on any lawful occupation, trade or business.' The Constitution also guarantees decent work under the following articles: Articles 25(1) on *slavery and servitude* and Article 25(2) on *forced labour* 'No person shall be held in slavery or servitude or be required to perform forced labour.' Forced labour does not include: any labour required in consequence of the sentence or order of a court; any labour required of any person while that person is lawfully detained which, though not required in consequence of the sentence or order of a court, is reasonably necessary in the interests of hygiene or for the maintenance of the place at which the person is detained; any labour required of a member of a disciplined force as part of that member's duties as such or, in the case of a person who has conscientious objections to service as a member of a naval, military or air force, any labour which that person is required by law to perform in place of that service; any labour required during any period when Uganda is at war or in case of any emergency or calamity which threatens the life and well-being of the community, to the extent that the requiring of the labour is reasonably justifiable in the circumstances of any situation arising or existing during the period or as a result of the emergency or calamity, for the purpose of dealing with that situation; or any labour reasonably required as part of reasonable and normal communal or other civic obligations;

(2) Article 29(1) on right to freedom of association. The Constitution of the Republic of Uganda, 1995 recognizes the right of individuals to form and join

183. Article 2 of the Constitution of the Republic of Uganda, 1995.

associations or unions, including trade unions and political or other civic organizations. Chapter four of the Constitution of the Republic of Uganda, 1995 provides that every person shall have the right to freedom of association, which shall include freedom to form and join associations, including trade unions and political and other civic organizations. The Constitution of the Republic of Uganda, 1995 also provides that every Ugandan has a right to participate in peaceful activities to influence the policies of government through civic organizations.

(3) Article 34(4) on protection of children from economic exploitation and hazardous work. 'Children are entitled to be protected from social or economic exploitation and shall not be employed in or required to perform work that is likely to be hazardous or to interfere with their education or to be harmful to their health or physical, mental, spiritual, moral or social development.'

(4) Article 39 on right to a clean and healthy environment. 'Every Ugandan has a right to a clean and healthy environment.' Article 40(1) right to work under satisfactory, safe and healthy conditions; equal pay for equal work without discrimination, rest and reasonable working hours and periods of holidays with pay and remuneration for public holidays; Articles 40(3) right to form and join trade union and Article 40(4) on protection of women during pregnancy and after birth, in accordance with the law.

(5) *Legislation*. Chapter six of the Constitution of the Republic of Uganda, 1995 establishes the legislative arm of government – Parliament, which is mandated to make laws on any matter for the peace, order, development and good governance of Uganda.[184] Legislation may be called various names; it may be called Statutes, Acts of Parliament, Promulgations or Decrees. Parliament may also delegate its law-making powers to other bodies, for instance, to a District Local Council, a City Council, a Municipal Council of a Sub-County Local Council or a government official, for instance, a Minister. These bodies or persons with delegated legislative powers make laws referred to as bye-laws, ordinances, rules or regulations.

(6) Labour law specifically mediates the relationship between workers, employing entitles, trade unions and the government. This means that the relationship between employee and employer or trade union and in this case 'sport clubs' can be mediated by labour law or Employment law in Uganda.

(7) Among the key labour laws in Uganda include, the Workers Compensation Act 2000, the Employment Act 2006, the Labour Unions Act 2006, the Occupational Health and Safety Act 2006 and the Labour Disputes (Arbitration and Settlement) Act 2006.

(8) In summary, the Employment Act 2006, outlines the conditions of employment including, contracts of service, termination of contracts, termination of notices, protection of wages, hours of work, rest and holidays, employment of women, employment of children and care of employees. The Employment Act, applies to all workers employed by an employer under a contract of service. However, it does not apply to: the Uganda Peoples' Defense Forces other than their civilian employees and employers and their dependent relatives when

184. Article 79(1) of the Constitution of the Republic of Uganda, 1995.

dependent relatives are the only employees in a family undertaking where the total number of dependent relatives does not exceed five. The Minister of Gender Labour and Social Development is mandated on consultation with the Labour Advisory Board to exclude from the application of all or part of this Act, limited categories of employed persons in respect of whom special problems of a substantial nature arise.[185]

(9) *Case Law.* The Courts of Law of Uganda apply the doctrine of precedent. This means that when deciding a case with facts similar to those of an earlier decided case, the courts decide the new case by following the principles of law set out and in the earlier decision. The earlier decided cases are what are referred to as precedents. The courts of precedent are the Supreme Court, Court of Appeal and the High Court. Decisions of a higher court are binding while those of the same court are persuasive. The law in Uganda governing employment in Uganda is the Employment Act, 2006. Several cases from the Industrial Court of Uganda have availed precedents that form part of the Case Law on Employment in Uganda.

(10) *Common Law and Doctrines of Equity.* Common law and doctrines of equity are observed by virtue of following the English legal system. Common law refers to decisions of English judges, which were based on the customs of the English communities.[186] Equity means fairness. Other maxims of equity include; he who comes to equity must come with clean hands, equity regards as done that which ought to be done, equity follows the law and delay defeats equity. Where the Ugandan laws do not provide a remedy, the common law and doctrines of equity are applied and only if they are not contrary to Uganda's written law.

(11) *Customary Law.* Customary law entails a number of customs followed by the different people of Uganda. Customary law is not written but entails the norms that are followed by people. For customary law to be followed it must not be repugnant to natural justice and not contrary to the Constitution of the Republic of Uganda, 1995. It is highlighted in the Constitution of the Republic of Uganda, 1995 that cultural and customary values, which are consistent with fundamental rights and freedoms, human dignity, democracy and with the Constitution, may be developed and incorporated in aspects of Ugandan life.[187] The Constitution of the Republic of Uganda, 1995 outlawed criminal customary law in Uganda.

A. *International Instruments*

172. International instruments on labour and human rights that have been ratified such as the International Labour Organization (ILO) where Article 1(1) is to the

185. Employment Act, 2006.
186. A Citizen's Handbook on Law & Administration of Justice in Uganda, Third edition, Judicial Service Commission, (2007) p. 3.
187. National Objective and Directive Principles of State Policy, Directive XXIV.

effect that all nations that have ratified the convention should undertake to suppress the use of forced labour. Uganda ratified this convention and thus is bound to it.

II. CBA

173. A central tenet, though not fully operational in Uganda, is the right to unionize and collectively bargain. This includes the option of industrial action to increase members' wages and improve working conditions. Labour rights are in context universal and apply to immigrant workers as well. From a practical trajectory, the existing regulatory policy in Uganda – an eight-hour workday and a forty-hour workweek – with extra hour's payable as overtime, remains one of the prime products of labour movement campaigns.[188] The labour Unions Act No 7/2006 and regulations SI 36/2006 are concerned with the establishment, registration and management of labour unions. Section 4 provides for the right of association of employees. Section 5 spells out offences that contravene the rights provided. Minimum Wages (advisory Boards and Councils) Act, Cap 221. Provides for the minimum wages advisory boards and wage councils. It further regulates remuneration and conditions of employment to employees. Section 14 lays down penalty for failing to pay minimum wage or comply with employment conditions.

174. Remuneration is determined according to the collective agreement. If there is no collective agreement in the sector of work, employees are entitled to reasonable remuneration. An employer must not pay remuneration that is less than stipulated in the collective agreement. Remuneration can contain various bonuses and such bonuses may include experience bonus, overtime pay and extra compensation for shift work among others. Any changes in an individual's salary should be notified to him/her in writing.

175. Apart from general work-related foci, labour rights also involve advocacy against child labour. In Uganda as elsewhere, child labour is viewed as exploitative and cruel, and often and deprives children the right to education. A report by the International Labour Organization (ILO) estimated that in 1998, 44.4% of children between the ages of ten and fourteen in Uganda were already working. One such group is the Elimination of Child Labor Trust Uganda (ECLATU), a private sector sponsored initiative to stamp out child labour in tobacco growing areas. The ILO leads the International Program on the Elimination of Child Labor (ILO-IPEC).

176. Under the labour law, employees are free to join labour unions of their choice. This freedom is guaranteed both under the Constitution and under the Labour Unions Act.

188. CCEDU: Labour Rights in Uganda. Available at: https://www.ccedu.org.ug/index.php/blog/36-labor-rights-in-uganda-a-summary-overview#:~:text=Among%20the%20key%20labor%20laws,the%20Occupational%20Safety%20Act%202006.

177. Article 29(e) of the Constitution of the Republic of Uganda, 1995 provides that every person shall have the right to freedom of association which includes freedom to form or join trade unions. Section 3 of the Labour Unions Act also provides that employees shall have a right to organize themselves in any labour union and may assist in running the labour union, bargain collectively through a representative of their own choice, withdraw their labour and take industrial action. Meanwhile, under section 4 the employer is barred by the Act from interfering with this right to associate otherwise if he does, he commits an offence under section 5 for which he is criminally liable. Labour unions are considered an important factor in the process towards more sustainable consumption and production patterns. They offer an organizational platform for a large number of workers and are involved in numerous policy processes. However, labour unions have traditionally focused their attention on job security and maintenance as well as workplace issues. Conversely, environmental concerns and sustainable development are usually not high on the political agenda of labour unions.

178. Though legal statutes appear well in place, challenges in implementation variously arise especially due to the lack of a cohesive trade union movement.

§2. Status of Players

179. Players as employees have the right to enter into contracts with the various sports associations which establish a legally binding relationship between them. Once a contract is established, the relationship between the players and the sports clubs becomes legal.

I. Professionals

180. A professional player is one who has a written contract with a club and is paid more than the expenses he effectively incurs or acquires non-monetary services or materials in return for his footballing activity.[189] A professional player can only sign a professional contract for one club irrespective of formation of the game, for avoidance of doubt a player signed by a club for eleven aside shall not sign for another beach soccer club or futsal and vice versa.[190] All non-Ugandan citizens can only be registered as professional players in the national leagues subject to acquisition of ITC in accordance to FIFA Rules on Status and transfer of players. A player's contracts shall be valid only if it is registered with FUFA in accordance with FUFA Document Bureau regulation.[191]

---

189. Article 5 of the FUFA Regulations on Status and Transfer of Players.
190. *Ibid.*
191. *Ibid.*

181. A contract of service (if not required by law to be in writing) may be made orally or in writing.[192] If it is made with an illiterate person, it shall be attested to by means of a written document drawn up by a magistrate or labour officer who shall before attesting first ascertain that the employee has freely consented to it, be satisfied that the employee has duly understood its terms, before accepting it, ensure that it is in conformity with the provisions of the Act.

182. It is clearly of value that the terms of a contract be reduced in writing or evidenced in writing. In this way, disputes can be averted more easily and evidence will be easier to obtain in the event of dispute. It is therefore a sensible step for the parties (or at least the employer who has the facilities) to be charged with the task of reducing the agreement in writing.

II. Amateurs

183. A player without a contract is defined as amateur and is free to transfer to any club of his/her choice at the end of the season.[193] An amateur player belongs to a club or academy for which he/she is registered until an ITC is issued or until he/she is registered with another club/academy.[194]

184. A professional player is one who has a written contract with a club and is paid more than the expenses he effectively incurs or acquires non-monetary services or materials in return for his footballing activity. All other players are considered to be amateurs.[195]

III. Others

185. A professional player is one who has a written contract with a club and is paid more than the expenses he effectively incurs or acquires non-monetary services or materials in return for his footballing activity. All other players are considered to be amateurs.[196]

§3. Employment Relationship

186. Employee contracts attribute rights and responsibilities between parties to a bargain and are made between the employer and the employee. It is governed by contractual principles such as offer, acceptance, consideration and legality.

192. Section 25, Employment Act 2006.
193. Schedule 1 of the FUFA Regulations on Status and Transfer of Players.
194. Article 5 of the FUFA Regulations on Status and Transfer of Players.
195. *Ibid.*
196. *Ibid.*

187. Rights and duties are superimposed on these contractual arrangements and employers cannot derogate from these rights or duties even by contract. The parties agree to the terms and conditions provided they are not less than what the Employment Act provides or exclude the application of a provision of the Act to the detriment of the employee.[197]

I. Employment Agreements

188. Sports Professionals may be engaged through a contract of service as an agreement between an employer and an employee or a contract for service, where an independent contractor, such as a self-employed person is engaged for a fee to carry out an assignment or project. The Employment Act provides that a contract of service means any contract whether oral or in writing, whether express or implied, where a person agrees in return for remuneration, to work for an employer and includes a contract of apprenticeship.[198]

189. Employee contracts attribute rights and responsibilities between parties to a bargain and are made between the employer and the employee. It is governed by contractual principles such as offer, acceptance, consideration and legality. Rights and duties are superimposed on these contractual arrangements and employers cannot derogate from these rights or duties even by contract. The parties agree to the terms and conditions provided they are not less than what the Act provides or exclude the application of a provision of the Act to the detriment of the employee, where permitted by the Act (section 27).

A. *Express Terms*

190. The express terms of the employment contract are the terms actually agreed on by the parties. Where the contract is written these terms will appear on the document, where it is oral, practical difficulties can arise in proving what was agreed. A contract of service (if not required by law to be in writing) may be made orally or in writing (section 25). If it is made with an illiterate sports person, it must be attested to by means of a written document drawn up by a magistrate or labour officer who shall before attesting first ascertain that the employee has freely consented to it, be satisfied that the employee has duly understood its terms, before accepting it, ensure that it is in conformity with the provisions of the Act.

191. It is clearly of value that the terms of a contract be reduced in writing or evidenced in writing. In this way, disputes can be averted more easily and evidence will be easier to obtain in the event of dispute. It is therefore a sensible step for the parties (or at least the employer who has the facilities) to be charged with the task

197. Section 27 of the Employment Act 2006.
198. Section 2 of the Employment Act 2006.

of reducing the agreement in writing. An employee is entitled to receive from his employer notice in writing of the particulars of employment.

192. It should contain: the full names and addresses of the parties to the contract, date of commencement of contract, job title, place where employees' duties are to be performed, wages which the employee is entitled to, employee's normal hours of work, etc. (section 59).

193. Where there is any dispute between the employer and employee as regards the terms and conditions of employment, these particulars shall serve as evidence (section 60). The general aim of the provision is to encourage the development of explicit and clear terms about the most important elements of the employee's contract.

B. Implied Terms

194. Frequently differences will arise about a matter on which the parties never reached actual agreement. When the contract was being made, they may never even have considered the matter or they may have done so briefly without reaching any conclusion. Court will not readily imply terms; generally, the parties themselves and not the judges should decide what terms they are contracting under. Terms may be implied by facts/officious bystander test, custom or by common law practices.

195. Terms Implied by facts/officious bystander test. A common form of implied term is one which is implied by virtue of the particular facts of the case. In deciding whether to fill a gap in the contract by implying a term, the test usually adopted is, if at the time they made their contract, would they almost certainly have agreed to the suggested term.

196. Implied terms by Custom and Practice. Some customs and practices prevailing at the workplace may be implied as terms of the employment contract, in order to attain contractual status in this manner, the alleged custom must satisfy four requirements: It must be notorious; certain; reasonable; and is a custom that is regarded as obligatory. In other words, the term must be: fair and not irregular, well established over a period of time, known to employees, clear and unambiguous. If the custom is not notorious, then it is impossible to say that the employee in question could have not been aware of it on being hired. As in the case of work rules, it is essential to demonstrate that employees should have been fully aware of the custom or rule.

197. Terms Implied by Common Law. These are more or less duties imposed by common law on the parties to a contract of employment. The common law duties on the part of the employer are to pay wages, to provide work, exercise care, to cooperate and to provide access to a grievance procedure. On the part of the employee, the debate is whether there is a duty to obey reasonable orders, exercise reasonable care and competence, maintain fidelity, i.e., be honest, not compete, not misuse confidential information, not impede the employer's business and duty to account. Most of these duties have been incorporated in written law.

C. *Probationary Agreements*

198. A probationary period can be agreed upon at the beginning of the contract of employment. However, this can as well depend on the organization's human resource policies. During this period, the employee can assess whether the work is suitable for the tasks performed and may dissolve the contract of employment without a period of notice. The grounds for dissolving the contract of employment during the probationary period must not be discriminating. During the probationary period, the employee is paid normal remuneration stated in the contract. The Employment Act restricts the tenure for probation.

D. *Employment of Non-citizens*

199. This is governed by The Uganda Citizenship and Immigration Control Act Cap 66 and The Uganda Citizenship and Immigration Control Regulations No 16/04. No person shall enter or remain in Uganda unless that person is in possession of a valid entry permit, certificate of permanent residence or pass issued under the Act.

200. A non-citizen shall not be issued with the above documents unless he possesses a passport, a certificate of identity, a convention travel document or any other valid travel document section 53)

201. Section 59 provides that a non-citizen shall not unless he/she possesses the above documents be employed in a parastatal or private body, public service, by a private person, engage in private business in Uganda.

202. There are classes of entry permits specified in the Act (section 54). Class G covers employees. The person must satisfy the immigration board that he has been offered and has accepted employment in Uganda.

E. *Employment of Children*

203. Children under 16 years of age are entitled to be protected from social or economic exploitation and shall not be employed in or required to perform work that is likely to be hazardous or to interfere with their education or to be harmful to their health or physical, moral, mental, spiritual or social development (Article 34 of the Constitution).

204. A child under the age of 12 years shall not be employed in any business, undertaking or work place (section 32 of the Employment Act). A child under the age of 14 is only allowed to be employed for light work carried out under the supervision of an adult aged over 18 years and which work does not affect the child's education. A child shall not be employed between the hours of 7 pm and 7 am. Any person including a labour union or employer's organization may complain to a labour officer if he or it considers that the child is being employed in breach of these provisions of the law.

II. Players' Obligations

A. Misconduct

205. The employee must not misconduct himself. The term misconduct includes persistent laziness, immorality, dishonesty, drunkenness etc. Misconduct will justify summary dismissal if it goes to the root of the contract. However, the misconduct may not necessarily be a once off but one where there is a history of complaints of insolence and inefficiency from time to time.

B. Obedience to Reasonable Orders

206. Generally, employers are not entitled to give orders regarding what employees do outside their working hours but there are some jobs which warrant giving certain instructions about what an employee should or should not do while not actually at work, orders regarding what an employee should do outside work will usually be regarded as unreasonable, unless the contract clearly envisaged giving those orders.

207. But the courts would be most reluctant to strike down instructions given about how a particular task should be performed since, by the nature of the employment relationship, it is for the employer to determine how the work is to be done. An order would have to be wholly unconnected with the employee's job or be manifestly unreasonable before it would be rejected by the courts.

C. Cooperation

208. Over and above the question of obeying specific orders, employees are subject to an overriding duty to cooperate with their employers in the performance of their work. Because the employment contract envisages a continuing relationship between employers and employees, it would seem that the employee must perform the various contractual obligations with a degree of good faith. It is an implied term that the contract should be performed in such a way as not to undermine its commercial objective.

D. Account for Property and Gain

209. And employee must account for any money or property belonging to his employer and any gains made thereon.

E. Trade Secrecy

210. The employee must maintain secrecy over his employer's affairs during the time of his employment. If the employer wishes to extend this beyond the period of employment, it would be advisable to insert a suitable clause in the contract of employment (restraint of trade clause). The employee is under an obligation to his employers not to disclose confidential information obtained by him in the course of, and as a result of his employment. The duty applies both during employment and afterwards, if the employee seeks to use such information to the detriment of his employer.

F. Competence and Care

211. An employee must be reasonably competent to perform the job for which he was hired.

III. Players' Rights

212. An employee is entitled once in every calendar year, to a holiday with full pay at the rate of seven days in respect of each period of a continuous four months' service or twenty days a year, to be taken at such time during such calendar year as may be agreed between the parties. Annual leave applies only to employees who have performed continuous service for their employer for a minimum period of six months or have been working under a contract of service for sixteen hours a week or more.

213. A female employee shall, as a consequence of pregnancy, have the right to a period of sixty working days leave from work on full wages.

214. When an employee's contract is terminated he or she is entitled to receive a holiday with pay proportionate to the length of service for which he or she has not received such a holiday, or compensation in lieu of the holiday.

215. An employee who has completed not less than one month's continuous service with an employer and who is incapable of work because of sickness or injury is entitled to sick pay, however, he or she should notify or cause to be notified as soon as is reasonably practicable, his/her employer of his/her absence and the reason for it; and produce, if requested by his/her employer a written certificate signed by a qualified medical practitioner certifying his/her incapacity for work and duration of the incapacity.

216. A male employee immediately after the delivery or miscarriage of his declared wife has the right to a period of four working days' leave from work annually.

217. An employee is required to work for an employer for not more than six consecutive days with a day's rest, taken on any day which is customary or agreed between the parties. The maximum number of hours per week is 48 h.

IV. Clubs' Obligations

A. Obligation to Provide Work

218. The employer is duty-bound to provide work to the employee.[199] Generally, while the employee is contractually obliged to attend at the workplace during the agreed times for working, the employer is not obliged to furnish actual work to be done. All that usually is required of the employer is to pay the agreed remuneration for the period during which the employee is at work. Although having no actual work to do may deprive the employee of job satisfaction is always regrettable but by itself provides no cause of action.

B. Obligation to Pay Wages

219. Wages are paid in legal tender to the employee entitled to payment.[200] The payment of wages is required to take place at the place of the employee's work or, if he or she works at more than one location, the premises of his/her employer from which he or she works or from which his/her work is administered. An employee is not entitled to receive wages in respect of any period where he or she is absent from work without authorization or good cause. Absence with good cause may be attributable to the occurrence of exceptional events preventing the employee from reaching his/her place of work or from working; summons to attend a Court of Law or any other public authority having power to compel attendance; or death of a member of the employee's family or dependent relative, subject to an agreed number of days' absence on any one occasion and a maximum of six days in any one calendar year among others.

199. Section 40 of the Employment Act.
200. Section 41 of the Employment Act.

C. Provide Safety

220. The employer must take reasonable care to ensure that his premises are safe. He will therefore be in breach of his duties if he provides defective safety equipment knowingly or which he should have known on reasonable examination. The burden is on him to examine the equipment. He will also be in breach if he fails to remedy breaches that have been brought to his attention.

221. Article 39 of the Constitution provides for the right to a clean and healthy environment. The Occupational Safety and Health Act imposes an obligation on employers to ensure the safety of employees at work. They are thus required to put in place measures for the achievement of this purpose, e.g., provision of protective gear against the effect of pollution, to monitor and control the release of dangerous substances into the environment, to supervise the health of workers who are exposed to dangerous hazards due to pollution and other harmful agents, e.g., through periodic medical examination, keeping medical records of workers, ensuring that work premises remain safe and without risk to health, displaying safety precautions etc. The Act requires workplaces to be kept in a clean state to have suitable lighting to ensure that buildings at a workplace are of sound construction, to have adequate supply of wholesome drinking water accessible to by all workers, adequate facilities for taking meals, a first aid room etc.

222. The administration and enforcement of the provisions of the Act are entrusted to the Commissioner for Occupational Health and Safety and inspectors. Their role is, with the assistance and cooperation of the occupier of the workplace to enter into work premises to ensure that employers are implementing the requirements of the Act. Orientation provides employees with necessary safety information about their job and tasks, informs them of specific details about workplace hazards and provides an opportunity to learn about the company and their colleagues, ask questions and to clarify new or confusing information. New employees starting with any entity will have expectations about the workplace culture and the emphasis on the safety orientation they receive will be reflected in their work performance, their eagerness to learn and their willingness to contribute to a safe and healthy workplace.

223. The *Workers Compensation Act 2000* entitles employees to automatic compensation for any personal injury from an accident arising out and in the course of his/her employment even if the injury results from the employee's negligence. The Workers' Compensation Act of Uganda is intended to ensure that sports players who get injured in the course of the employment receive compensation from their employers. The Act defines an employer as the Government of Uganda, any person incorporated or unincorporated, association or partnership, which directly engages a worker or which, in respect of any worker, carries on the business of hiring out his/her services.

224. The Act applies to all employment within Uganda and to workers employed by or under the Uganda Government in the same way and to the same extent as if the employer were a private person, but not to active members of the armed forces. Workers' compensation is a legal remedy that covers medical expenses and wage loss for employees who have been injured in the course and scope of their employment. An employee must report any work-related injury or illness to the supervisor immediately or other personnel of the organization.

225. If personal injury by accident arises out of and in the course of a worker's employment, the injured worker's employer shall be liable to pay compensation in accordance with this Act.[201] Any personal injury by accident arising while the employee is travelling directly to or from his/her place of work for the purpose of employment shall be deemed to be an accident arising out of and in the course of his/her employment.[202] It shall be or the employee who suffers injury by accident arising while travelling to or from his/her place of work to show that such travel was direct. Compensation shall be payable whether or not the incapacity or death of the worker was due to the recklessness or negligence of the worker or otherwise.[203] Any accident arising in the course of employment shall, unless the contrary is proved, be presumed to arise out of employment. Because of this liability, the Act requires every employer to insure and keep himself/herself insured in respect of any liability which he or she may incur under the Act to any worker employed by him/her.

226. The word 'injury' is defined to include an accident and a disease mentioned under the Act;[204] the injury may be a fatal one or it may be one of a temporary or permanent nature, which incapacitates a worker for any employment which he or she was capable of undertaking at the time when the accident occurred. If the worker is killed as a result of an accident for which the employer has liability under this Act, the dependants (if any) of the deceased may recover from the employer the expenses of medical treatment of the deceased, burial of the deceased and expenses incidental to the medical treatment and burial of the deceased.[205]

227. In *Tatyabula v. SOC SMG & Another*,[206] the plaintiff Sospeter Tatyabala through M/s Ekirapa & Co. Advocates filed this suit against the defendants jointly and severally for compensation for injuries sustained during the performance of his duties, breach of his contract of employment, unfair termination, special, exemplary and general damages, interest and costs of the suit. Sometime in November 2005, the plaintiff was recruited by the second defendant and underwent training in order to go and work in Iraq as a contract guard. Subsequently, the plaintiff was contracted by the first defendant on 8 April 2006 to work as a non-combatant security guard for twenty months and was posted to Iraq vide an overseas third country nationals contract. The plaintiff carried on his work with due diligence and to the

201. Section 3 of the Workers Compensation Act.
202. Section 3(4) of the Workers Compensation Act.
203. Section 3(6) of the Workers Compensation Act.
204. Section 1 of the Workers Compensation Act Cap. 225.
205. Section 4(6) of the Workers Compensation Act Cap. 225.
206. High Court Civil Suit No. 174 of 2008.

satisfaction of the defendants until the night of 17 February 2007 when he developed a painful swelling on the right side of his back which he reported to the platoon commander/leader. On 19 February 2007, the plaintiff was informed that his services had been terminated and accordingly was deported to Uganda on 4 March 2007. Upon arrival in Uganda, the plaintiff underwent medical treatment at Bambi Medical consultants and later went for surgery at Mulago hospital for chronic traumatic brusitis of an adventitious bursa overlaying the inferior aspects of the scapula, which is caused by, repetitive strain/sheering injury. As a result, the plaintiff was left permanently incapacitated to the tune of 17%. The Judge observed that the disease suffered by the plaintiff, i.e., bursitis is one of the scheduled diseases. Therefore, under section 29 of the Workmans' Compensation Act, the employer was liable to pay compensation to the employee for the disease so contracted. Compensation is arrived at by multiplying his salary for sixty months by the percentage of disability, which in the instant case is $1000 \times 60 \times {}^{17}/_{100}$, which equals to USD 10,200, which amount was accordingly award to the claimant.

228. In *National Council for Sports v. Peter Grace Sseruwagi,* court considered the employment relationship where Peter was on 21 December 1967 appointed as a full-time coach with the National Council of Sports. When Peter Grace Sseruwagi reported to the National Council of Sports an injury on his back while in USA on 5 July 1984 during the Olympic Games, he claimed for compensation for the injuries sustained as a result of that accident. Court noted that since the claim was brought 19 years after it had occurred, the claim was time-barred.

D. Indemnity

229. The employer must indemnify his employee where the employee has incurred a liability while acting on the employer's behalf except where the employee knew that he was doing an unlawful act.

E. Employer's Liability under Workman's Compensation

230. If personal injury by accident arises out of and in the course of a worker's employment, the injured worker's employer shall be liable to pay compensation in accordance with this Act.[207] An act shall be deemed to be done out of and in the course of employment when a worker acts to protect any person on the employer's premises whom the worker believes to be injured or imperilled, or when a worker acts to protect property on the employer's premises.

231. Any personal injury by accident arising while the employee is travelling directly to or from his/her place of work for the purpose of employment shall be deemed to be an accident arising out of and in the course of his/her employment. It

207. Section 3 of the Workers' Compensation Act.

shall be for the employee who suffers injury by accident arising while travelling to or from his/her place of work to show that such travel was direct. Compensation shall be payable under this section whether or not the incapacity or death of the worker was due to the recklessness or negligence of the worker or otherwise.

232. Any accident arising in the course of employment shall, unless the contrary is proved, be presumed to arise out of employment. Because of this liability, the Act requires every employer to insure and keep himself/herself insured in respect of any liability which he or she may incur under the Act to any worker employed by him/her.

F. Confidentiality of Medical Information

233. Medical information about individual staff members is to be treated confidentially. The organization will take reasonable precautions to protect such information from inappropriate disclosure.

G. Obligation to Provide Medical Insurance

234. This is especially important for injuries that might be sustained during the sports activities. For instance, starting 2020, FUFA has offered medical insurance to all the players in Uganda Premier League. This caters for injuries to players and compensation for permanent disabilities as a result of injuries. It was observed that over the years some players had sustained career-threatening injuries and clubs failed to help them recover fully. The insurance arrangement caters for over four hundred (400) players.[208] FUFA also offers medical insurance to delegates, FUFA staff, Uganda Cranes' players and players featuring in the FUFA Juniors League. This arrangement is catered for by the National Insurance Company (NIC).[209]

V. Termination of Contract

235. In recognition of the frequent dismissals of employers from work especially in the Ugandan private sector, the framers of the Employment Act came up with major safeguards against both unlawful or unfair termination and unlawful dismissal. The Act provides for certain requirements that must be complied with before a contract of service can be terminated. The one loophole in the Act is failure to make a clear distinction between termination and dismissal, the Act appears to use

208. FUFA medical insurance to UPL players commences in 2020 Available at: https://sportsoceanuganda.com/2019/12/30/fufa-medical-insurance-to-upl-players-commences-in-2020/ (Accessed 13 Mar. 2022).

209. FUFA medical insurance to UPL players commences in 2020 Available at: https://sportsoceanuganda.com/2019/12/30/fufa-medical-insurance-to-upl-players-commences-in-2020/ (Accessed 13 Mar. 2022).

the two words interchangeably. 'Termination of Employment' means the discharge of an employee from an employment at the initiative of the employer for justifiable reasons other than misconduct, such as expiry of contract, attainment of retirement age. On the other hand, 'Dismissal from Employment means the discharge of an employee from employment at the initiative of his or her employer when the said employee has committed verifiable misconduct.' An employment contract can be terminated in a number of ways which include the following (section 65 of the employment Act): the contract can be terminated by the employer with notice, where it is a contract of service, being a contract for a fixed term of task, ends with the expiry of the specified term or the completion of the specific task (unless it is renewed), Where the contract is ended with or without notice on the part of the employee as a consequence of unreasonable conduct on the part of the employer towards him, Where the contract is ended by the employee in circumstances where the employee has received notice from the employer but before the expiry of that notice.

236. A contract of service shall not be terminated by an employer unless he or she gives notice to the employee except, where the contract of employment is summarily terminated in accordance with section 69 of the employment Actor where the reason for termination is attainment of retirement age (section 58). The notice must be in writing and shall be in a form and language that the employee to whom it relates can reasonably be expected to understand. The period of notice depends on the period for which the worker has been employed and the notice periods are specified under the Act. No employer has the right to terminate a contract of service with less notice than that to which the employee is entitled by any statutory provision or contractual term (section 69(2). However, nothing shall prevent an employee from accepting payment in lieu of notice.

237. An employer shall before reaching a decision to dismiss an employee on grounds of misconduct or poor performance explain to him the reason for dismissal in a language the employee may reasonably be expected to understand. The employee is entitled to have another person of his/her choice present during the explanation. The employer shall in turn give the employee a hearing and consider any representations which the employee and the person if any chosen by him may make. Whether the dismissal is a summary dismissal which is justified or whether it is a fair dismissal, the employer must have given the employee a reasonable time within which to prepare these representations. Where these requirements are not complied with, the employee may lodge a complaint with the labour officer for redress (section 66).

238. Irrespective of whether any dismissal which is a summary dismissal is justified or whether it is fair an employer who fails to comply with this section is liable to pay the employee a sum equivalent to four weeks net pay (section 66(4)).

A. *Unfair Reasons for Termination*

239. Notwithstanding the above, it is vital to note that not all reasons that the employer may give are fair reasons to justify termination of a contract. Thus, under section 75 of the Act, a list of reasons which may be considered as unfair is given, i.e., A female employee's pregnancy or any reason connected with her pregnancy, the fact that an employee took, or proposed to take, any leave to which he was entitled to under the law or a contract, an employee's membership or proposed membership of a labour union, participation or proposed participation in the activities of a labour union outside working hours, or with the consent of the employer within working hours, an employee's refusal or proposed refusal to join or withdraw from a labour union, an employee's race, sex, colour, religion, political union or affiliation, nationality, social origin, marital status, HIV status or disability, an employee's temporary absence from work for any period up to 3 months or reliable grounds including illness or injury, An employee's initiation or proposed initiation of a complaint or other legal proceedings against his employer. The organization or intended organization of a strike or other form of industrial action where the strike of industrial action is lawful (section 76).

B. *Summary Dismissal*

240. An employer is entitled to dismiss summarily and the dismissal shall be termed justified where the employee has by his/her conduct indicated that he has fundamentally broken his obligations under the contract of service (section 69). This would arise from serious misconduct being manifested by the employee. Summary dismissal is deemed to have taken place when the employer terminates the service of an employee without notice or with less notice than that to which the employee is entitled by any statutory provision or by a contractual term. This is a new provision because formerly summary dismissal meant only dismissal without notice. Where the employment contract does not specify the grounds for summary dismissal what constitutes serious misconduct for these purposes depends on the nature of the job in question and the terms of the contract. Certain actions almost invariably would be regarded as a serious misconduct, like deliberately destroying the employer's property, stealing from the employer and gross insubordination.

241. In *Eletu v. Uganda Airlines Corporation*, it was held that 'at common law, to justify such dismissal, a breach of duty must be serious one, a breach amounting in effect to repudiation by the servant of his obligations under the contract of employment such as disobedience of lawful orders, drunkenness, immorality, assaulting fellow workers, incompetence and neglect.' 'There is no fixed rule of law defining the degree of misconduct which would justify summary dismissal. However, summary dismissal is a strong measure to be justified only in exceptional circumstances. The test to be applied in determining whether a summary dismissal was justified is whether misconduct leading to summary dismissal goes to the root of the contract so as to indicate unwillingness to continue to be bound by the original terms of the contract.'

242. In a nutshell, players and coaches may be employees to a given sports club under a contract, and the above Ugandan labour laws relatively apply to them during their course dealing as they also apply in other aspects. This is because 'Athlete and coach employment' is also recognized as ordinary employment in Uganda and therefore labour and employment laws of Uganda apply to them under sports law.

§4. Agents' Regulations

243. An agent is a person who acts on behalf of another. In Uganda, these are referred to as intermediaries. An intermediary means any person or legal persons (e.g., company, business) who, for a fee or free of charge, is engaged by a club (being any club that is registered or affiliated with FUFA/FIFA, one of its member federations or an association affiliated to one of its member federations) and/or player in a 'transaction'.[210] A transaction means the conclusion of either: an employment contract between a player and club, including, without limitation, a renegotiation, variation, extension or renewal of an existing employment contract, or a transfer agreement between two clubs.[211]

I. Regulations

244. Only an intermediary may be used and paid by a player or club in relation to any Intermediary Activity. Alternatively, a player or club may represent themselves in any matter relating to a transaction. A player or club must not use or pay any person for Intermediary Activity unless that person is registered as an intermediary and is entitled to act under a valid Representation Contract. An intermediary must not carry out any Intermediary Activity in the place of, or on behalf of, or as agent or representative of, any person other than the player and/or the club he is engaged to act for.

245. A club, player, intermediary or other participant must not so arrange matters as to conceal or misrepresent the reality and/or substance of any matters in relation to a transaction. Furthermore, parties to a transaction are prohibited from: proposing in any way, either directly or indirectly, to any other party to the transaction that the transaction is dependent upon a player's agreement to contract with a specific intermediary; or making the transaction conditional on the player's agreement/contract with a specific intermediary. To this end, an intermediary, club and player must ensure that all relevant contracts and documents contain the name, signature and registration number of each and every intermediary carrying out any Intermediary Activity in relation to a transaction (whether directly or indirectly), as well as any information as may be required by FUFA from time to time. If a player

210. Article 2(2) of the FUFA Regulations on Working with Intermediaries.
211. *Ibid.*

or club has not used the services of an intermediary at any time in a transaction, this fact must be stated in all relevant documents in respect of such transaction.[212]

246. In order for an intermediary to represent a player, the intermediary and player or a club (as applicable) must have entered into a validly executed written Representation Contract prior to that intermediary carrying out any Intermediary Activity on his or its behalf. The Representation Contract must contain the entire agreement between the parties in relation to the Intermediary Activity, and shall, at a minimum, contain all Obligatory Terms of the relevant Standard Representation Contract. The parties may add other terms so long as they are consistent with the Obligatory Terms of the Standard Representation Contract and the requirements of the FIFA Regulations on Working with Intermediaries. More so, all parties to a Representation Contract must ensure that copies of any and all Representation Contracts to which they are a party to are lodged with FUFA in any manner as may be prescribed from time to time. Representation Contracts must be lodged within ten days of being executed and in any event no later than at the time of the registration of a transaction by FUFA.

A. *Eligibility to Register as Intermediary*

247. In order to register with FUFA as an intermediary, you ought to be a natural legal person who wishes to act as an intermediary. The registration once completed is valid for one year. A natural person seeking to register as an intermediary is required to sign declarations and satisfy FUFA of his impeccable reputation before such registration will be accepted, on terms that shall be stipulated by FUFA in its Test of Good Character and Reputation for Intermediaries. As such, intermediaries are obliged to notify FUFA within ten working days of any change in circumstances relating to the requirements of the Test of Good Charter and Reputation for Intermediaries. A natural person whose registration is rejected at this stage or an intermediary whose registration is suspended due to a change in his circumstances may appeal to FUFA Appeals Committee, however, a compensation payment and/or any Solidarity Payment and/or Training Compensation payment will not be applicable to such appeals. FUFA will approve the natural person's registration or revoke the suspension of the registration (as applicable) but shall not have any liability of any nature to this natural person arising out of, or in connection with, any decision or action taken or omitted by FUFA in relation to the natural person's registration or the determination of the same.[213]

B. *Registration Conditions*

248. As soon as the intermediary has completed his registration with FUFA, he will be entitled to use the following designation, and no variation thereof, after his

212. Article 3 of the FUFA Regulations on Working with Intermediaries.
213. FUFA Regulations on Working with Intermediaries.

name in business relations: 'FUFA Registered Intermediary'. An intermediary shall not be entitled to hold himself out as having any connection with FUFA other than this designation (for the avoidance of doubt, the usage of FUFA's crest by the intermediary is prohibited).[214] An intermediary must procure that the organization with which he is associated complies with any requirement of FUFA pursuant to its Rules and regulations.[215]

C. Requirements Relating to Minors

249. Prior to entering into a Representation Contract with a minor or with a club in respect of a minor, an intermediary must get from FUFA additional authorization to deal with minors. This authorization can be applied for by an intermediary when registering with FUFA in accordance with schedule I or at any point after his registration. This authorization shall be valid for three years, subject to the intermediary remaining registered. A legal person registering as an intermediary cannot apply to deal with Minors. An intermediary applying to deal with Minors shall be required to satisfy FUFA of his suitability, on terms that shall be stipulated by FUFA from time to time.

D. Legal Persons Registered as Intermediaries

250. A legal person can only be registered as an intermediary by a natural person already registered as an intermediary. A legal person registered as an intermediary shall be responsible for declaring (within the form prescribed by FUFA from time to time those natural persons registered as intermediaries who are authorized to conduct Intermediary Activity on behalf of the legal person. Any Intermediary Activity carried out on behalf of a legal person registered as an intermediary must be carried out by a natural person registered as an intermediary and authorized to represent the legal person. When a legal person registered as an intermediary carries out Intermediary Activity for or on behalf of a player, coach and/or a club in a transaction, the name, signature and registration number of the natural person representing said legal person must appear on all relevant paperwork as is required by FUFA from time to time. When a legal person registered as an intermediary is involved in a transaction, FUFA will publish the name of the natural person declared as representing the legal person in the said transaction.[216]

214. *Ibid.*
215. *Ibid.*
216. *Ibid.*

II. Rights

251. If there is a term of a Representation Contract that breaches the requirements of the FIFA Regulations on Working with Intermediaries, it shall not be permitted. In such cases, FUFA has the power to notify the parities of any such breach whereupon the parties shall remedy the breach by making the necessary amendments as notified. All parties to a Representation Contract must inform FUFA in writing in case of any early termination, novation, variation or other event that effects the validity or status of a Representation contract (save for the natural expiry of the Contract), within ten days of such event.

252. Where a player has a Representation Contract with an intermediary, a club must deal with the intermediary in relation to any transaction concerning the player unless the player provides a prior written request to the club requesting it not to do so, such written request also to be provided by the player to the intermediary as soon as reasonably practicable and in any event prior to the transaction taking place.[217]

253. When it comes to remuneration, an intermediary may be remunerated by the club or the player for whom he acts. Payment must be made in accordance with the terms of either the Representation Contract between the parties or the relevant paperwork submitted to FUFA to register the transaction.

254. Where an intermediary undertakes Intermediary Activity for a player, the player may discharge his obligations to pay the intermediary as specified in either the Representation Contract between the parties or the relevant paperwork submitted to FUFA to register the transaction in one, more, of the following ways only: the player may pay the intermediary directly; and/or only where the player makes a request in writing to the club, the club may: make an actual deduction in periodic instalment(s) from a player's net salary in favour of the intermediary, so that the sums are deducted and paid in discharge of the player's obligation to the intermediary contained in the relevant Representation Contract or the relevant paperwork submitted to FUFA; and/or discharge the player's liability towards his intermediary, as contained in the relevant Representation Contract or the relevant paperwork submitted to FUFA, on the player's behalf as a taxable benefit.[218]

255. With regard to commission, where the intermediary and the player agree in the Representation Contract that a commission (either by way of lump sum or by instalments) is to be paid in respect of a transaction, it shall be calculated on the basis of the player's Basic Gross Income as set out in the employment contract concluded by the player in respect of which he/she was represented by the intermediary.[219]

---

217. *Ibid.*
218. *Ibid.*
219. *Ibid.*

256. Where the intermediary and the player agree on periodic instalments and the player's employment contract in respect of which he was represented by the intermediary lasts longer than the Representation contract, the intermediary is entitled to the agreed instalments after expiry of the

257. Representation Contract, until the player's employment contract expires or, if earlier, until the player signs a new employment contract without the involvement of that intermediary.[220]

258. Any and all remuneration or payments of whatever nature, and howsoever arising, and whether direct or indirect, made to any person in relation to any Intermediary Activity for and on behalf of the club, must be made by the club only, and must be fully recorded in the accounting records of the club. This however does not prevent an Intermediary acting for a club from paying another Intermediary with whom he/she has assigned or subcontracted any Intermediary Activity duties or services or responsibilities.[221]

259. Where the Intermediary and the club agree that such a commission is to be paid, they shall also agree in the Representation Contract what the commission shall be and whether the club shall remunerate the Intermediary with a lump sum payment at the start of the employment contract of the player who was the subject of the transaction or whether the club will pay by periodic instalments and/or whether such commission (or any instalment or part thereof) shall be conditional in any way.[222]

III. Obligations

260. Where an intermediary assigns or subcontracts any Intermediary Activity duties or services or responsibilities in relation to a player or a club to another intermediary, the intermediary is required to: lodge a copy of the Representation Contract between the assigning or subcontracting intermediary and the player or club in accordance with FUFA Document Registration Regulations; record the terms upon which those obligations are assigned or subcontracted and incorporate the written consent of the player or club in a single document; and complete and lodge the Document in the same way as for a Representation Contract under FUFA Document Registration Regulations.[223]

261. Additionally, an intermediary must not, either directly or indirectly, make any approach to, or enter into any agreement with, a player in relation to any Intermediary Activity before the 1st day in January of the year of the player's 16th birthday. The intermediary cannot enter into a Representation Contract with a Minor

220. *Ibid.*
221. *Ibid.*
222. *Ibid.*
223. *Ibid.*

unless it is countersigned by the Minor's parent or legal guardian with parental responsibility and approved by FUFA. By the same token, an intermediary can only enter into a Representation Contract with a player for a maximum duration of two years.[224]

262. An intermediary, or an Intermediary's Organization, must not pass any remuneration directly relating to Intermediary Activity to any other person. This does not affect the ability of an Organization to pay its employees or contractors pursuant to their employment or other contracts or any other parties for purposes unrelated to any Intermediary Activity.[225]

263. Clubs shall ensure that payments to be made by one club to another club in connection with a transfer, such as transfer compensation, training compensation, or solidarity contributions, are not paid to intermediaries and that the payments is not made by intermediaries. This includes, but is not limited to, owning any interest in any transfer compensation or future transfer value of a player/coach. The assignment of claims is also prohibited.[226]

264. Players or clubs that engage the services of an intermediary when negotiating an employment contract and/or a transfer agreement are prohibited from making any payments to such intermediary if the player concerned is a Minor.[227]

265. As a recommendation, players, clubs and intermediaries may adopt the following benchmarks: The total amount of remuneration per transaction due to intermediaries who have been engaged to act on a player's behalf should not exceed 15% of the player's Basis Gross Income for the entire duration of the relevant employment contract. The total amount of remuneration per transaction due to intermediaries who have been engaged to act on a club's behalf in order to conclude an employment contract with a player should not exceed 15% of the player's/coach's eventual Basic Gross Income for the entire duration of the relevant employment contract. The total amount of remuneration per transaction due to intermediaries who have been engaged to act on a club's behalf in order to conclude a transfer agreement must not exceed 15% of the eventual transfer compensation paid in connection with the relevant transfer of the player or coach officials as defined by the FUFA Statute are prohibited from receiving any payment from an intermediary of all or part of the fees paid to that intermediary in transaction. Any official who contravenes these requirements is subject to disciplinary sanctions.

266. Players or clubs are required to disclose to FUFA or their respective Associations the full details of any and all agreed remunerations or payments of whatsoever nature and that they have made or that are to be made to an intermediary. Players or clubs must in particular reach agreements with the intermediary to ensure

---

224. Article 4 of the FUFA Regulations on Working with Intermediaries.
225. FUFA Regulations on Working with Intermediaries.
226. FUFA Regulations on Working with Intermediaries.
227. *Ibid.*

that there are no obstacles to the disclosure of the above-mentioned information and documents. The above-mentioned contracts must be attached to the transfer agreement or the employment contract, as the case may be, for the purpose of registration of the player. Clubs or players are required to ensure that any transfer agreement or employment contract concluded with the services of an intermediary bears the name and signature of such an intermediary. In the event that a player or a club has not used the services of an intermediary in their negotiations, the pertinent documentation lodged within the scope of the respective transaction shall contain a specific disclosure of this fact.[228]

267. FUFA is entitled to publish the name and registration number of every intermediary, as well as where applicable, the name of the organization (or a legal person registered as an intermediary) he is connected with. FUFA is also entitled to publish, in any manner and at any time it considers appropriate, a list of every transaction in which any intermediary has been involved. FUFA is by the same token entitled to publish, in any manner and at any time it considers appropriate, the total consolidated amount of a club, player, intermediary or other Participant, therefore a club, player, intermediary or other Participant must not so arrange matters as to conceal or misrepresent the reality and/or intermediaries. Furthermore, FUFA is entitled to publish any decision made pursuant to the FUFA Working with Intermediaries Regulations, in any manner and at any time it considers appropriate, including the name and any other relevant information relating to an intermediary in respect of whom a disciplinary decision has been made, including where a registration is suspended or withdrawn. This is in addition to FUFA's powers to publish contained in the General Provisions Relating to Inquiries, Commissions of Inquiry, Regulatory Commissions of FUFA, Other Disciplinary Commissions, Appeals Boards and Safeguarding Review Panel Hearings, or elsewhere in its Rules and regulations.[229]

268. When it comes to consent to Dual/Multiple Representations, prior to engaging the services of an intermediary. players or clubs shall use reasonable endeavours to ensure that no conflict of interest exists or are likely to exist either for the players or clubs or for the intermediary. An intermediary must only act for one party to a transaction. An intermediary may undertake Intermediary Activity for more than one party in relation to a transaction, only where the following requirements are met in full: the intermediary has a pre-existing Representation Contract with one party to the transaction ('the first party') and the Representation Contract has been lodged with FUFA in accordance with the requirements of FUFA Document Registration Regulations; alternatively the Intermediary has entered into a subcontract agreement in relation to the first party in accordance with the requirements of FUFA Document Registration Regulations; and the Intermediary obtains all parties' prior written consent to him providing services to any other party to the transaction ('the other party(ies)') in the form prescribed by FUFA from time to time; and once the Intermediary and the other party(ies) have agreed terms, (but prior to them entering

228. *Ibid.*
229. *Ibid.*

into a Representation Contract), the Intermediary must inform all parties in in writing and/or in the form prescribed by FUFA from time to time of the full particulars of the proposed arrangement's including, without limitation, the proposed fee (if any) to be paid by all parties to the intermediary; and all parties are given the reasonable opportunity to take independent legal advice and/or, in the case of a player, to take advice from the Professional Footballers' Association prior to providing written consent in the form prescribed by FUFA from time to time; and having been given such opportunity, all parties provide their express written consent for the Intermediary to enter into a Representation Contract with the other party on the proposed terms in the form prescribed by FUFA from time to time.[230]

269. In scenarios where consent is withheld, in accordance with the above requirements, the Intermediary is not permitted to proceed with the provision of services to the other party(ies) or to receive any remuneration from the other party(ies) in respect of the relevant transaction, and the other party(ies) are not permitted to receive any services from the Intermediary or make any payment to the Intermediary in respect of the relevant transaction. The intermediary may continue to represent the first party (only) in respect of the relevant transaction and be paid for such services in accordance with this Regulation and the terms of the relevant Representation Contract.[231]

270. With regard to restrictions on conflict of interest an intermediary or an Intermediary's Organization cannot have an interest in a club. Similarly, a player, club official or manager shall not have any interest in the business or affairs of an Intermediary's Organization.[232]

271. Such interest shall be defined as: beneficial ownership of more than 5% of any entity, firm or company through which the activities of the club or intermediary (as applicable) or conducted and/or being in a position or having any association that may enable the exercise of a material, financial, commercial, administrative, managerial or any other influence over the affairs of the club or intermediary (as applicable) whether directly or indirectly and whether formally or informally. An interest includes an interest of: A Spouse, Child, Stepchild, Parent or Sibling of The intermediary, player, club, club official or manager (as applicable). A company in which any legal or beneficial interest or any proportion or share is held by the intermediary, spouse, child, stepchild, parent or sibling of the intermediary, player, club, club official or manager (as applicable) (save for holding of less than 5%) and/or a company over whose affairs financial, commercial, administrative, managerial or any other control or influence can be exercised by the individual or any spouse, child, stepchild, parent or sibling of the intermediary, player, club, club official or manager (as applicable). An intermediary must not have, either directly or indirectly, any interest of any nature whatsoever in relation to a registration right or an

230. *Ibid.*
231. *Ibid.*
232. *Ibid.*

economic right. This includes, but is not limited to, owning any interest in any transfer compensation or future transfer value of a player. This does not prevent an intermediary acting solely for a club in a transaction being remunerated by reference to the total amount of transfer compensation generated by this transaction.[233]

272. To guarantee that the intermediaries remain ethical, an intermediary must not give, offer or seek to offer, any consideration of any kind, either directly or indirectly, to any club, club official, manager, coach or player as a result of, or in connection with, a transaction or in return for any benefit, service, favour or any kind of preferential treatment in respect of the club's coach, players, access to those players or the promotion of the intermediary's services with those players. clubs, club officials, managers and players are prohibited from accepting such offers or receiving such consideration. Similarly, an intermediary must not give, offer or seek to offer, any consideration of any kind, either directly or indirectly, to a player/coach (or any family member of that player/coach) in relation to entering into a Representation Contract with that intermediary. Players/coaches are prohibited from accepting such offers or receiving such consideration.[234]

273. A duty of disclosure is bestowed upon a player, coach, club, club official or manager who must disclose to FUFA any agreement or contractual or other arrangement, whether formal or informal that exists between any players, coach, club, club official or manager and any intermediary (or an Intermediary's Organization) whereby any money is paid by or on behalf of such intermediary (or such intermediary (or such intermediary's organization) to such player, coach, club, club official or manager. Such disclosure must be within ten days of the intermediary entering into such a contractual or customary arrangement with the players, coach, club, club official or manager. Additionally, an intermediary must disclose to FUFA any agreement or contractual or other arrangements whether formal or informal that exist between that intermediary and any club official, manager or club in respect of a club official or manager or club in respect of a club official or manager whereby such intermediary represents the interests of any such club official, manager or club in respect of a club official or manager. Such disclosure must be made within ten days of: the intermediary entering into such an agreement or contractual or other arrangement with a club official, manager or club in respect of a club or manager; or an individual becoming a club official or manager and having a pre-existing agreement or contractual or other arrangement with an intermediary; or a person registering becoming as an intermediary and having a pre-existing agreement or contractual or other arrangement with a club, a club official, manager or club in respect of a club official or manager.[235]

274. Intermediaries, players, coaches, clubs, club officials and managers must also disclose in writing any actual or potential conflict of interest they might have in relation to a transaction and ought to obtain the express written consent of the

233. *Ibid.*
234. *Ibid.*
235. *Ibid.*

other parties involved in the matter (in the form prescribed by FUFA from time to time) in order for their activity in the transaction to continue. A copy of this form shall be disclosed to FUFA within ten days of being completed and in any event no later than at the time of the registration of a transaction by FUFA.[236]

275. Any breach of these provisions amounts to Misconduct in accordance with FUFA Disciplinary code and FUFA Ethics Code. Any charge for Misconduct shall be dealt with in accordance with the Rules of FUFA Disciplinary code or FUFA Ethics Code and shall be determined by the judicial bodies of FUFA.[237]

IV. Employment and Economic Dispute Settlements

276. The Employment Act provides for ways on how employee grievances can be handled for example where an employer neglects or refuses to fulfil the terms of a contract of employment, or where a complaint or a labour dispute arises as to the rights or liabilities of either party under a contract of employment.

277. The Industrial Court was established under the Labour Disputes (Arbitration and Settlement) Act, 2006, Laws of Uganda. The Court's jurisdiction ambit are labour disputes referred to it by a party to a dispute where a labour officer has failed to dispose of the dispute within eight weeks under the court's regulations as requested under the act,[238] disputes referred by the Labour officer at the request of the party or on the officer's own volition when is unable to resolve the dispute; or by responsible Minister[239] on notice of an intended withdrawal of labour within five days. Appeals can also be filed against labour officers' decision under the Employment Act. The Industrial Court has no original jurisdiction over Labour disputes.

§5. Social Security

278. This is governed by the National Social Security Fund Act[240] (NSSF Act) and is regarded as the principle or practice or a programme of public provision (as through social insurance or assistance) for the economic security and social welfare of the individual employee and his/her family. It applies to all employers in Uganda including those in the Sports field. Sports Associations can as well have in-house social security programmes for their employees. The main purpose is retirement planning.

236. *Ibid.*
237. *Ibid.*
238. Section 5 of the Labour Disputes (Arbitration and Settlement) Act, 2006.
239. Section 27 the Labour Disputes (Arbitration and Settlement) Act, 2006, Laws of Uganda.
240. Cap. 222 Laws of Uganda.

I. Legal Framework

279. The NSSF Act allows any employee of or above the age of 16 and below the age of 55 years as eligible for registration and membership to the Fund. Subject to any prescribed terms and conditions, the employer may apply for voluntary registration as a contributing employer; and any eligible employee of such employer may thereafter apply for voluntary registration as a member of the fund.

280. Under the NSSF Act,[241] every contributing employer is required for every month during which he or she pays wages to an eligible employee to pay to the fund, within fifteen days next following the last day of the month for which the relevant wages are paid, a standard contribution of 15% calculated on the total wages paid during that month to that employee.

281. If an eligible employee is employed successively or concurrently by two or more employers, each of such employers shall pay to the fund in respect of such employee a contribution corresponding to the wages he or she pays to such eligible employee.[242] This would apply to sports personalities employed at both national and club levels.

282. An employer is required to furnish to the managing director on an approved form particulars regarding each eligible employee in his/her service, his/her wages, the contribution due on such wages, the total wages.

283. A new initiative of Voluntary Membership which provides employers and workers that are not compelled by the mandatory provisions of the NSSF Act the opportunity to voluntarily save for their retirement has been launched. This is open to employers with less than five employees and individuals who are former NSSF members, whom the Fund already paid their respective benefits, but are still able and willing to save with the Fund.

II. Specific Conditions Applied to Sport

284. The 2021 NSSF Amendment Act has widened the definition of employer to include any a company registered or incorporated under the Companies Act, 2012. The national sports association falls squarely within this definition.

285. The 2021 NSSF Amendment Act introduces section 20A which allows access to an amount not exceeding 20% of the midterm benefits that have accrued from contributions made to the Fund. Members who are 45 years of age and above and have made contributions to the fund for at least ten years are eligible for the midterm benefits above. Persons with disability are also eligible for midterm access

241. Section 12, National Social Security Fund Act Cap 222 Laws of Uganda.
242. Section 11(3) National Social Security Fund Act Cap 222 Laws of Uganda.

amounting to 50% of their accrued benefits, provided they are 40 years of age and above and have made contributions to the Fund for at least ten years.

286. This is particularly relevant to sports personalities who may choose to retire early or those forced to retire due to an injury that causes a disability.

Part IV. Doping and Sport

Introduction

287. Doping is referred to as the use of a substance(s) that could have the effect of artificially improving or reducing the player's physical and/or mental condition and so augmenting artificially his athletic performance. The use of unacceptable substances and drugs is such an escalating vice among sportsmen men worldwide. The Uganda Olympic Committee highlights that Uganda subscribes to the world anti-doping code of 2021.

§1. Legal Framework

I. The World Anti-Doping Code

288. The World Anti-Doping Code International Standard Prohibited List of 2021 provides for prohibited substances and methods to wit: anabolic agents – some of which may be found, without limitation, in medications used for the treatment of, e.g., male hypogonadism. Peptide hormones, growth factors, related substances, and mimetic – some of which may be found, without limitation, in medications used for the treatment of, e.g., anaemia, male hypogonadism, growth hormone deficiency. Beta-2 agonists – some of which may be found, without limitation, in medications used for the treatment of, e.g., asthma and other respiratory disorders. Hormone and metabolic modulators – some of which may be found, without limitation, in medications used for the treatment of, e.g., breast cancer, diabetes, infertility (female), polycystic ovarian syndrome. Diuretics and masking agents some of these substance(s) may be found, without limitation, in medications used for the treatment of, e.g., heart failure, hypertension.[243]

289. The World Anti-Doping Code International Standard Prohibited List of 2021 prohibits the following processes: the administration or reintroduction of any quantity of autologous, allogenic (homologous) or heterologous blood, or red blood cell products of any origin into the circulatory system. Artificially enhancing the uptake, transport or delivery of oxygen including, but not limited to: perfluoro chemicals; efaproxiral (RSR13) and modified haemoglobin products, e.g.,

243. World Anti-Doping Code 2021 Available at: https://www.wadaama.org/sites/default/files/resources/files/2021_wada_code.pdf (Accessed 23 Feb. 2022).

haemoglobin-based blood substitutes and microencapsulated haemoglobin products, excluding supplemental oxygen by inhalation. Any form of intravascular manipulation of the blood or blood components by physical or chemical means is also prohibited.[244]

290. When it comes to Chemical and Physical Manipulation the following are prohibited: Tampering, or Attempting to Tamper, to alter the integrity and validity of Samples collected during Doping Control.

291. Including, but not limited to: Sample substitution and/or adulteration, e.g., addition of proteases to Sample. Intravenous infusions and/or injections of more than a total of 100 mL per 12-hour period except for those legitimately received in the course of hospital treatments, surgical procedures or clinical diagnostic investigations.[245]

292. With regard to Chemical and Physical Manipulation, the following, with the potential to enhance sport performance, are prohibited: the use of nucleic acids or nucleic acid analogues that may alter genome sequences and/or alter gene expression by any mechanism. This includes but is not limited to gene editing, gene silencing and gene transfer technologies. The use of normal or genetically modified cells is also forbidden.[246]

293. Stimulants some of which may be found, without limitation, in medications used for the treatment of, e.g., anaphylaxis, attention deficit hyperactivity disorders (ADHD), cold and influenza symptoms are forbidden. Narcotics some of which may be found, without limitation, in medications used for the treatment of, e.g., pain, including from musculoskeletal injuries. Cannabinoids, Glucocorticoids – some of which may be found, without limitation, in medications used for the treatment of, e.g., allergy, anaphylaxis, asthma, inflammatory bowel disease. P1 Beta blockers – some of which may be found, without limitation, in medications used for the treatment of, e.g., heart failure, hypertension are also forbidden.[247]

II. Ordinary Legislation

A. The National Drug Policy and Authority Act

294. No person is permitted to mix, compound, prepare, supply or dispense any restricted drug unless that person is a registered pharmacist, medical practitioner,

244. World Anti-Doping Code 2021 Available at: https://www.wadaama.org/sites/default/files/resources/files/2021_wada_code.pdf (Accessed 23 Feb. 2022).
245. World Anti-Doping Code 2021 Available at: https://www.wadaama.org/sites/default/files/resources/files/2021_wada_code.pdf (Accessed 23 Feb. 2022).
246. World Anti-Doping Code 2021 Available at: https://www.wadaama.org/sites/default/files/resources/files/2021_wada_code.pdf (Accessed 23 Feb. 2022).
247. World Anti-Doping Code 2021 Available at: https://www.wadaama.org/sites/default/files/resources/files/2021_wada_code.pdf (Accessed 23 Feb. 2022).

dentist or veterinary surgeon or a licensed person.[248] No person is permitted to supply any narcotic drugs under international control other than for medical, dental or veterinary purposes.[249] No person can have in his/her possession without lawful excuse, the proof of which shall lie on him/her, any narcotic drug or psychotropic substance under international control.[250] These are the same drugs utilized for doping.

B. The Narcotic Drugs and Psychotropic Substances (Control) Act, 2016

295. The Possession of, and trafficking in, narcotic drugs and psychotropic substances as well as their cultivation is prohibited and a person who has such substances in their possession commits an offence attracting up to twenty-five years of imprisonment.[251]

296. The prohibited narcotic drugs include the following:

'Acetorphine (3-0-acetyltetrahydro-7x-(1 hydroxy-1-methylbutyl)-6, 14-endotheno-oripavine); Acetyl-alpha-methylfentanyl(N-[1-(a-methylphenethyl)-4-piperidyl] acetanilide); Acetylmethadol (3-acetoxy-6-dimethylamino-4, 4-diphenylheptane); Alfentanil-(N-[1-[2-(4-ethyl-4, 5-dihydro-5-oxo-1IH-tetrazol-lylethyl) (methoxymethyl)-4-piperidinyl]-Nphenylpropanamide monohydrochloride) Allylprodine (3-ally-1-methyl-4-phenyl-4-propionoxypiperidine); Alphacetylmethdol (alpha-3-acetoxy-6-dimethylamino-4, 4-diphenylheptane); Alphameprodine (alpha-3-ethyl-l-methyl-4-diphenyl-4 propionoxypiperidine) Alphamethadol (alpha-6-dimethylamino-4, 4-diphenyl-3-heptanol) Alpha-methylfentanyl (N-[1-(a-methylphenethyl)-4-piperidyl] propionanilide); Alpha-menthylthiofentanyi (N-[1-[1-methyl-2-(2-thinenyl-4-piperidyl] propionanilide); Alphaprodine (alpha-1, 3-dimethyl-4-phenyl-4-propionoxy piperidine); Anileridine (1-para-aminophenethyl-4-phenylpiperidine-4-carboxylic acid ethyl ester); Benzethidine (1-(2-benzyloxyethyl)-4-phenylpiperidine-4-carboxylic acid ethyl ester); Benyimorphine (3-benzimorphine); Betacetylmethadol (beta-3-acetoxy-6-dimethylamino-4, 4-diphenylheptane); Beta-hydroxyfentanyl (N-[1-(beta-hydroxyphenethyl)-4-piperidyl] propionanilide); Beta-hydroxy-3-methylfentanyl (N-[1-beta-hydroxyphenethyl)-3-methyl-4-piperidyl] propionanilide); Betameprodine (beta-3-ethyl-l-methyl-4-phenyl-4-proplonoxypiperidine); Betamethadol (beta-6-dimethylamino-4, 4-diphenyl-3-heptanol); Betamethadine (beta-1, 3-dimethyl-4-phenyl-4-propionoxypiperidine) Bezitramide (1-(3-cyano-3, 3-diphenylpropyl)-4-(2-oxo-3-propionyl-l-benzimidazolinyl)-piperidine). Cannabis (Indian Hemp) and

248. Section 13 of the National Drug Policy and Authority Act.
249. Section 26(2) of the National Drug Policy and Authority Act.
250. Section 47(1) of the National Drug Policy and Authority Act.
251. Section 4 of the Narcotic Drugs and Psychotropic Substances (Control) Act, 2016.

Cannabis resin (Resin of Indian Hemp) Clonitazene (2-para-chlorbenzzyl-1-diethylaminoethyl-5-nitrobenzimidazole) Coca Leaf, Cocaine (methyl ester of benzolecgonine), Codoxime (dihydrocodeinone-6-carboxymethyloxime), Concentrate of poppy straw (the material arising when poppy straw has entered into a process for the concentration of its alkaloid when such material is made available in trade).'[252]

III. Sports Regulations

A. FUFA Regulations on Status and Transfer of Players

297. When it comes to soccer in Uganda, the player and the club are subjected to all anti-doping regulations dully in existence in the game of soccer. Doping is the usage of substances and the forbidden methods featuring on the list of the pertinent bans. Doping is forbidden. Whoever manages illegal substances or encourages encourage use of banned drugs shall be sent to FUFA Disciplinary Committee.[253]

298. Doping is strictly forbidden by the FUFA, CAF & FIFA and any person found to have indulged in doping shall be sanctioned according to the FIFA regulations. The FUFA medical committee and/or RADO may randomly ask players without prior notice to provide their organic substance samples for the doping tests. Any player who refuses to instantly provide such samples shall be liable for disciplinary action.

B. FUFA Competition Rules

299. Doping is the use of a substance(s) that could have the effect of artificially improving or reducing the player's physical and/or mental condition and so augmenting his athletic performance artificially. Doping is strictly forbidden by the FUFA, CAF & FIFA and any person found to have indulged in doping shall be sanctioned according to the FIFA regulations. The FUFA medical committee and/or RADO may randomly ask players without prior notice to provide their organic substance samples for the doping tests. Any player who refuses to instantly provide such samples shall be liable for disciplinary action.[254]

300. Many International sporting bodies, including the World Football governing body (FIFA) have come up with policies and campaigns to halt the use of these drugs among sportsmen.

---

252. Second Schedule of the Narcotic Drugs and Psychotropic Substances (Control) Act, 2016.
253. Article 12 of the FUFA Regulations on Status and Transfer of Players.
254. Article 7 of the FUFA Competition Rules.

IV. Sports Courts

A. *Court of Arbitration for Sport*

301. In accordance with the relevant provisions of the FIFA Statutes, any appeal against a final and binding FUFA/FIFA decision shall be heard by the Court of Arbitration for Sport (CAS) in Lausanne, Switzerland, unless another Arbitration Tribunal has jurisdiction in accordance with Article 73. CAS shall not, however, hear appeals on violations of the Laws of the Game, and suspensions of up to four matches or up to three months (with the exception of doping decision), or decisions which are appealable to an independent and duly constituted Arbitration Tribunal of an Association or Confederation.[255]

302. The Uganda Olympic Committee (UOC) in conjunction with the Regional anti-doping agency (RADO) for the East African region led, and coordinate the doping prevention efforts in the country. The FUFA Ethics Committee is the FUFA Judicial Body that is mandated to investigate and adjudge matters related to Ethics & Integrity in sports administration, doping, forgery and falsification, bribery, corruption, non-discrimination, offering and acceptance of gifts and other benefits, integrity of matches and competitions.

303. Despite the development of advanced drug testing systems, both deliberate and inadvertent doping in sports is increasing in elite, amateur and school sports [1–4]. According to the 2013 World Anti-doping Agency (WADA) report, the number of abnormal test findings recorded by anti-doping authorities worldwide have increased by more than 20% since 2012. In a bid to deter athletes from using banned performance enhancing drugs/methods, athletes have been subjected to impromptu in- and out-of-competition screening tests for these substances over time, and those athletes who test positive are given heavy punishments or fines. However, despite the rigorous testing procedures, the decades of doping scandals that have nonetheless prevailed have shown that the tests are no guarantee of a drug-free race.

V. Case Law

304. There has not been much litigation around doping in Uganda. However recently, a footballer, Samuel Ssenkoomi was found guilty of using banned substances and slapped with a one-year ban.[256]

---

255. Article 75 of the Statutes of the Federation of Uganda Football Associations (FUFA).
256. David Isabirye, 'Anti-doping in sports should be a brave, collective fight, says stakeholders', https://kawowo.com/2018/05/08/anti-doping-in-sports-should-be-a-brave-collective-fight-says-stakeholders/.

Part V. Sport and Commerce

Introduction

305. Commercialization of sports in Uganda is inhibited by the lack of enabling laws and not lack of the right mindset among the stakeholders in the sports sector. The National Council of Sports Act 1964 promotes sports merely as a form of recreation and physical exercise. It was suggested that there is a need to amend the current sports legislation to create a more conducive environment for the commercialization of sports. The National Council of Sports Act in its current form is obsolete and ought to be amended to bring it in line with the prevailing times. The National Council of Sports Act has not prevented the sports sector from attracting commercial investments/activities. There are a great deal of sponsorship deals signed, players committed to contracts, sports institutions merchandising their products, advertisement of sports events, crowds thronging sports events, and so forth.

§1. Public Law

306. The entertainment value of sport is being exploited to stimulate the industry into commercialization. Consequently, even though the National Council of Sports Act does not expressly recognize sports as a commercial activity, it does not prohibit its commercialization. There are presently some other legislations that can be relied upon to accelerate the commercialization of the Sports industry in Uganda:

I. The Contracts Act, 2010

307. A contract is a legally binding agreement. It represents a meeting of minds between the parties. Contracts in sports are subjected to similar principles of contracting like any other form of agreement. Most contracts, especially in amateur sports, like is the case in Uganda, are verbal and not reduced into writing. This should not be a cause for concern because the Contracts Act affords protection for both oral and written contracts and can be used to ensure the performance of obligations in sports.

II. The Companies Act, 2012

308. The Companies Act regulates the registration and management of companies. Sports clubs can take advantage of this legislation to institutionalize by incorporating as companies. Once incorporated, they take on the form of artificial beings capable of undertaking commercial activities such as owning property, executing contracts, instituting suits et cetera in their names as opposed to the current situation where officials enter transactions in their names on behalf of the clubs/ institutions. Incorporation also allows for clarity of ownership of these clubs and creates clear administrative structures.

III. The Employment Act, 2006

309. Professional athletes, coaches, medical personnel, grounds men, club managers, CEO, stewards to mention but a few are all employees of a particular sporting organization and are covered under the normal employment laws. Sports cannot, therefore, be isolated from employment laws.

IV. Intellectual Property Laws

310. Intellectual property rights are at the very centre of huge commercial opportunities in the sports industry. Intellectual Property Laws offer protection for patent rights, copyright, trademarks, and image rights which are very critical in the commercialization of sports especially in this era of televised sports and mass innovation in the industry. The legal protection offered under the Intellectual Property Laws helps secure the economic value of sports which in turn stimulates growth in the sector. Sporting business transactions related to sponsorships, merchandising, broadcasting and media deals are all fabricated around Intellectual Property Rights and Protection.

A. Copyright

311. According to the *Copyright and Neighboring Rights Act*, Copyright law grants authors, artists and other creators protection for their literary and artistic creations, generally referred to as 'works'. The kind of works protected by copyright include, but not limited to: literary and artistic works such as, novels, poems, plays, newspapers, adverts, films, musical compositions, choreography, paintings, drawings, photographs, sculptures and architecture, maps, technical drawings and computer software, programmes and databases. The expression authors' rights refer to the creator of an artistic work, its author, thus underlining that, as recognized in most laws, authors have certain specific rights in their creations that only they can exercise, which are often referred to as moral rights, such as the right to prevent distorted reproductions of the work. Other rights, such as the right to make copies, can be exercised by third parties with the author's permission, for example, by a publisher who obtains a licence to this effect from the author.[257]

B. Trademark

312. According to the *Trademarks Act 2010*, a trademark is a distinctive sign that identifies certain goods or services produced or provided by an individual or a company from those of other enterprises. A Trademark may consist of any word, symbol, design, slogan, logo, sound, smell, colour, label, name, signature, letter, numeral or any combination of them and should be capable of being represented graphically. The Trademark has to be distinctive, non-descriptive and not likely to cause confusion. The Trademark owner has the exclusive rights to prevent others from using the same or confusingly similar mark.[258]

C. Utility Models

313. According to the *Industrial Property Act 2014*, a Utility Model is an exclusive right granted by the government for an innovation/invention, which is either a product or process that offers a new technical solution to a problem. A product or process that is new and is useful can be protected using this system. Their term of protection is ten years. Registration for a utility model is simple and fast, and gives the holder the right to exclude others from exploiting the protected innovation/invention.[259]

314. Utility Models provide protection for incremental improvements to products and processes and it is very relevant for SMEs. For example: printing-roller cleaning system, fruit sorting machine, simple bottle cleaning machine etc.[260]

D. Patents

315. According to the *Industrial Property Act 2014*, a patent, like a utility model, is an exclusive right granted by the government for an invention. Protected inventions can range from simple things like a safety pin to sophisticated items like juice processing machine. An invention that is Novel, Inventive and is industrially applicable may be granted using a Patent. The term of protection for patents is twenty years. For the patent to remain in force the patent holder is required to pay annual maintenance fees.[261]

---

257. The Copyright and Neighbouring Rights Act.
258. The Trademarks Act 2010.
259. Part XII of the Industrial Property Act, 2014.
260. *Ibid.*
261. Part III of the Industrial Property Act, 2014.

E. Industrial Design

316. According to the *Industrial Property Act, 2014*, an Industrial Design is defined as the ornamental or aesthetic aspect of a useful article (product). The design may consist of three-dimensional features, such as the shape or surface of an article, or two-dimensional features, such as patterns, lines or colour.[262]

317. An industrial design in simple terms is the appearance of a product, it's what makes a product attractive and appealing to a consumer's eye. Industrial designs are applied to a wide variety of products of industry and handicraft items: from packages and containers to furnishing and household goods, from lighting equipment to jewellery, and from electronic devices to textiles. Industrial designs may also apply to graphic symbols and graphical user interfaces (GUI). Industrial design rights are granted for five years renewable for two more consecutive five-year term.[263]

V. Geographical Indication

318. According to the *Geographical Indications Act, 2013* a geographical indication (GI) is a sign used on products that have a specific geographical origin and possess qualities or a reputation that are due to that origin. In order to function as a GI, a sign must identify a product as originating in a given place. In addition, the qualities, characteristics or reputation of the product should be essentially due to the place of origin. Since the qualities depend on the geographical place of production, there is a clear link between the product and its original place of production.[264]

319. A geographical indication right enables those who have the right to use the indication to prevent its use by a third party whose product does not conform to the applicable standards. For example, in the jurisdictions in which the Darjeeling geographical indication is protected, producers of Darjeeling tea can exclude use of the term 'Darjeeling' for tea not grown in their tea gardens or not produced according to the standards set out in the code of practice for the geographical indication. However, a protected geographical indication does not enable the holder to prevent someone from making a product using the same techniques as those set out in the standards for that indication. Protection for a geographical indication is usually obtained by acquiring a right over the sign that constitutes the indication.[265]

262. Part XIII of the Industrial Property Act, 2014.
263. Industrial Property Act, 2014.
264. Geographical Indications Act 2013.
265. *Ibid.*

A. Media and Television Rights

320. The global obsession with footballers has created one of the great money spinners of the entertainment industry. In return for captivating audiences with their skills on the pitch, international soccer stars are now earning many more millions of dollars off the pitch being on television and other media, associating themselves with products from soft drinks to vehicles and airlines.

321. In today's modern sporting world, image rights can hold enormous commercial value to both the professional athlete and his club. Image rights can be defined as the proprietary rights that arise from the commercial exploitation of a sporting personality's name and image. Sports image rights are very valuable assets.

322. In a football context, image rights are simply the right a player possesses to control, sell, licence and otherwise monetize his/her likeness – that is, his/her image, name, nickname, voice, signature and all other characteristics unique to the player. Image rights are broadly defined, using the expression 'image' not in its narrow sense of 'likeness' but in its wider sense of 'persona' or 'brand', to use a marketing term.

323. All media rights in respect of the tournaments are the property of FUFA. No club can own individual media rights in respect of the Uganda Cup.[266]

B. Sponsoring

324. Clubs shall reserve the right to acquire their own sponsorship provided that any such sponsorship shall not in any way infringe with FUFA's Uganda Cup Commercial and Media Rights. For avoidance of doubt, all sponsorship contracts between clubs and potential sponsors shall be cleared by the FUFA Marketing Committee before they are signed by any competition club.[267]

325. The High Court of Uganda recently adjudicated a dispute regarding sponsorship in *Odongo v. FUFA Super League Ltd & Anor.*[268] In this case, the plaintiff alleged that on 19 November 2014 he made contact with a one Mr. Torrington by e-mail about sponsorship of elite competitions such as boxing and football so as boost their market viewership. The plaintiff alleged that through tireless efforts by way of negotiations and brokerage acumen secured the approval of all club owners and the Board FUFA Super League, that resulted in a sponsorship deal executed between the board of FUFA Super League, club owners and Azam Media t/s Azam TV for exclusive rights to sponsor, name, cover, air and/or broadcast, live telecasts of the FUFA Super league.

266. Uganda Cup Regulations 2019–2020.
267. *Ibid.*
268. (CIVIL SUIT NO. 244 OF 2015) [2019] UGHCCD 41 (20 Feb. 2019).

326. The sponsorship package to a tune of USD 1,900,000 was agreed over a period of three and a half years seasons effective February 2015. The plaintiff further contended that the first defendant at all material times had urged the plaintiff to carry on the negotiations with Azam Media and intimated that it would execute a formal agreement but it reneged on this promise. It was the plaintiff's case that the defendants intimated that he would promptly receive his 10% commission or USD 190,000 for a period of three and a half years. The first defendant denied any agreement between themselves and the plaintiff and contended that the plaintiff was privy to the contract executed between the first defendant and second defendant. The first defendant specifically denied any contract between themselves and the plaintiff.

327. The first defendant was approached by the second defendant about a sponsorship deal with Azam TV and as a result, the first defendant picked interest in the arrangement and the second defendant procured.

328. Court held that conversely, parties who want to enforce an oral agreement must take measures to document the existence of an oral agreement in the event the other party decided to not uphold their obligations. The plaintiff totally failed to prove his entitlement to any commission arising out of the purported oral contract between himself and the second defendant. The plaintiff's case failed and was dismissed with costs to the defendants.

C. Merchandising

329. Marketing rights are the property of FUFA. They include but are limited to the following: the Uganda Cup Title Naming Rights and Trademarks Designation Rights; use of the Uganda Cup Trophy Imagery; compound use clubs logos of participating clubs/teams; advertising on the right hand sleeve of each Uganda Cup referee in action; advertising on the right hand sleeve of all players of all participating clubs/teams; advertising on the right hand breast of all players of all participating clubs/teams; advertising on 100% of the pitch side perimeter at all Uganda Cup matches; production and sale of Uganda Cup branded materials; exclusivity of sale of services and/or products at Uganda Cup events; branding at all press conferences, interviews, and other press engagements. Branding of the FUFA ICT infrastructure.

330. Club/Team commercial rights in respect of the Uganda Cup are as follows: branding of club jerseys (midriff of the shirt) and other sports gear; branding of club ICT infrastructure; branding of club vehicles, publications and stationary; use of the Uganda Cup trophy by the current Champion club; stadium branding (if owned/ leased by club). This does not include pitch side branding and the stadium interior.

D. Ownership of Clubs

331. There are four types of club ownership and each club aligns its ownership by choosing one of the four models. These models include: institutional, privately owned, community-based and hybrid clubs.

332. Institutional Clubs: The Institutional clubs are 100% owned by a government institution that is created by an act of Parliament or a Government parastatal. This model is principally set up as a Public Relations and/or Corporate Social Responsibility (CSR) tool for the institution. These clubs are Uganda Revenue Authority, Kampala Capital City Authority (KCCA), Uganda People's Defence Forces (UPDF), Police and BUL.

333. Private Clubs: Private clubs are owned by a shareholding of natural and/or legal persons. This model is principally set up for football business purposes. Such clubs include Mbarara City, Bright Stars, Vipers, Wakiso Giants, Malaba Youth Development Association (MYDA), and Onduparaka. Mbarara City is 100% owned by the Western region youth Member of Parliament Mwine Mpaka Rwamirama.

334. Community Clubs: Community clubs are owned by a membership of more than 100 or so fans. This model is setup for sport but has proven most suitable for posterity and sports business. The current community clubs in Uganda are: Express FC (owned by Express Sports Club Limited), SC Villa (owned by Sports Club Villa Limited).

335. Hybrid Model: Hybrid model clubs normally have a compromise position of various inherited ownership, challenging to find suiting governance model practices. There are two hybrid clubs in Uganda: Kyetume and Busoga United. Kyetume has elements of private and institution. Reuben Mubiru Kaggwa Kimera has the majority shares (60%), Hogi Nsubuga (21%), Kyetume CBHC Programme (15%), Henry Titus Kayondo (3%) and David S. Kikabi with 1%. Busoga United's majority shareholder is Dinah Hope Nyago with 51% shares. The Jinja Secondary School board comes second with 35%. Busoga Kingdom, Dr. Joseph Muvawala, Fredrick Gume Ngobi, Godfrey Bwire Osodo, Daniel Oketch, Robert Adotu and Samuel Mugabi all have 2% each.

§2. PRIVATE REGULATIONS

336. Sports associations endeavour to abide by the public regulations on sports and commerce and are not at liberty to create their own rules.

Part VI. Sport and COVID

Introduction

337. The impact of COVID-19 could have been underestimated, the closure of economies rippled down the sports activities in Uganda. The first case of COVID-19 in Uganda was registered on 22 March 2020.[269] The government was first to respond; it introduced a number of restrictions on movements including the introduction of night curfews to curb the spread of the virus and maintain order during the lockdown period. The ban on movement of people, non-cargo vehicles and the closure of offices and businesses except essential services was introduced. Schools, churches, sports training fields and all other public places where large groups of people often congregate were shut.[270] It is important to recognize that COVID-19 is not just a health problem; it is also a social and economic issue. Its impact continues to be more severe among the most vulnerable, poor communities who often have no social safety nets to fall back to. It has particularly been difficult for people residing in slums, as there is massive space crunch, which makes it tougher to maintain social distance.[271] The Corona Virus Disease-2019 (COVID-19) has continued to spread across the world leaving death and economic devastation in its wake. Although the number of confirmed cases in Uganda remains very low in comparison to other countries, the containment adopted to curb the spread of the virus have affected business operations.[272]

338. This virus has continued to spread across the world following the first infections in Wuhan city in Hubei province of China in December 2019. According to WHO (2020), as of 9 May 2020, over 280,000 coronavirus-related deaths had been registered globally, with more than 4 million laboratory-confirmed COVID-19 cases, portraying not only the alarming levels of spread of the virus but also its severity. The World Health Organization (WHO) declared COVID-19 a global pandemic on 11 March 2020. Given its geographical spread, the pandemic is projected to have devastating effects on the global economy. Uganda has 1,29,578 cumulative cases with 3,317 cumulative deaths and 98,589 cumulative recoveries.[273] According to the IMF global economic Outlook, the world economy is projected to contract

269. https://www.sportanddev.org/en/article/news/slum-youth-during-pandemic Accessed 1 Feb. 2022.
270. *Ibid.*
271. *Ibid.*
272. Corti Paul Lakuma et al., How has the COVID-19 Pandemic impacted Ugandan Businesses? Results from a business climate survey, Special issue No. 01 May, 2020.
273. https://covid19.gou.go.ug/statistic s.html Accessed 28 Feb. 2022.

sharply by 3% in 2020 as a result of the pandemic. In the same vein, the Sub-Saharan African economy is expected to contract by 1.6%. UNECA (2020) shows that African businesses are being severely impacted by the COVID-19 crisis. Four out of five businesses in Africa are significantly affected by the current COVID-19 crisis, rating the effect as highly severe or severe. The proportion of severity is relatively uniform across the size of enterprises and the sector of business.[274]

§1. Governmental Measures

339. Upon registering its first case, the government of Uganda came up with a number of containment measures to curb the spread of the virus in the country, such as the closure of schools, restrictions on internal and international travel, wearing of protective gear, use of hand sanitizer and lockdown.[275] Whereas these measures were intended to enforce social distancing among the people, they affected the economy in various ways. For instance, due to border closures, the economy suffered from supply chain disruptions and reduction of visitors who contribute to revenue in the tourism sector. Sports activities were not to go as planned because many of the sportsmen and women were not in a position to move from one place to another. Many importers, traders and consumers in Uganda were also seriously affected. The effect is more severe among the small-scale business and traders because they earn their livelihood trading products such as textiles whose importation was suspended. There are reports of private employers laying off and effecting salary reductions of workers to cut down their costs and also deal with the loss of market opportunities/demand arising from extending the lockdown duration.[276] Whereas the measures introduced by the government of Uganda helped contain the rapid spread of the virus, measures including social distancing greatly impacted the communities, leading to severe mental health problems.[277] By social distancing, this meant that the different sports activities could not be carried out as planned since most of these activities, including football, rugby, swimming to mention but a few, involve body contact among the participants. The government has encouraged Ugandans to embrace the COVID-19 mass vaccination programme. The nationals were initially hesitant to get the vaccines because of social and religious beliefs which hindered their participation. Ugandan Health Minister Jane Ruth Aceng also noted that mass vaccination programme has been slowed down by the global shortage of vaccines because the demand outweighs production. Aceng says the Ugandan government has issued a list of vaccines that can be used in the country,

274. Corti Paul Lakuma et al, How has the COVID- 19 Pandemic impacted Ugandan Businesses? Results from a business climate survey, Special issue No. 01 May, 2020.
275. Corti Paul Lakuma et al, How has the COVID- 19 Pandemic impacted Ugandan Businesses? Results from a business climate survey, Special issue No. 01 May, 2020.
276. Corti Paul Lakuma et al, How has the COVID- 19 Pandemic impacted Ugandan Businesses? Results from a business climate survey, Special issue No. 01 May, 2020.
277. Youth Sports Uganda and their experiences of the pandemic. Available at: https://www.sportanddev.org/en/article/news/youth-sport-uganda-and-their-experiences-pandemic (Accessed 1 Feb. 2022).

including AstraZeneca, Johnson and Johnson, Pfizer-BioNtech, Sinopharm, Sinovac, Sputnik V, Sputnik Light and Moderna, adding that the Health Ministry officials are doing everything possible to obtain vaccine.[278] According to Ugandan health authorities, vaccinating priority groups such as teachers helped reopen schools for more than about 10 million pupils and students who had not been to school for 18 months because learning institutions were suspended so as to control the spread of the virus. After successful vaccination of the eligible population of children aged 12 to 18 years old has taken place, the universities and tertiary institutions have also since resumed business while observing the standard operation procedures. . With the increased rate of vaccination of teachers, the country hopes to stabilize more as schools were reopened at the end of 2021.[279]

340. The pandemic saw a number of changes impacting societies and countries as a whole, including the postponement of the Olympics, which had never happened in their history. Uganda, which had been experiencing a surge in cases, sent a nine-member squad to the Olympics, all of whom have been fully vaccinated. The Uganda Olympics Committee disclosed that members of the Ugandan Team tested positive for COVID-19, and one of the members was asymptomatic and being looked after by the health authorities in Izumisano city. They however confirmed that the rest of the team was well and continued to adapt in Izumisano.[280]

341. The small and medium businesses have experienced the largest effects of the risk associated with COVID-19 compared to large-scale businesses. The decline in small and medium businesses is due to inability to cope containment measures instituted by the government. Corti Paul Lakuma et al. state that nine out of ten businesses reported to have experienced an increase in operating expenses due to preventive measures instituted by the government to curb the spread of the virus. Agriculture enterprises have been worst hit due to challenges of accessing inputs arising from transport restrictions and the ban on weekly markets. In addition, prices of agricultural outputs have declined due to lost demand and the shift from consumption of fresh agricultural produce to dry rations.[281] Corti Paul Lakuma et al. reported in 2020 that 55% of the businesses reported to have experienced a moderate increase in the price of inputs. It is notable that the majority of the businesses in agriculture (43%) reported having experienced a decline in the price of input during the period. This could have been as a result of a fall in demand, which coincided with a build-up of inventory. On the other hand, inputs of manufacturing businesses have become relatively expensive largely due to disruption in the global supply chains, owing to closure of factories abroad. The pandemic has not affected prices of inputs in the northern region, but drove up prices in the western region,

---

278. https://www.voanews.com/a/covid-19-pandemic_uganda-lifts-some-covid-19-restrictions/6208989 .html (Accessed 1 Feb. 2022).
279. https://kiu.ac.ug/news-page.php?i=ministry-of-education-and-sports-confirms-increased-covid-19-vaccination-among-teachers Accessed 1 Feb. 2022.
280. Tokyo 2020: second member of Uganda @s Olympics delegation tests positive in Japan https://www.bbc.com/sport/africa/57579612.
281. Corti Paul Lakuma et al, How has the COVID- 19 Pandemic impacted Ugandan Businesses? Results from a business climate survey, Special issue No. 01 May, 2020.

particularly for businesses in food and recreation and mechanical services. Kampala and the Central region have only experienced a moderate increase in the price of inputs, particularly for mechanical services and industry for the case of Kampala, and trade and social services, such as health, for the Central region. On the other hand, the majority of the businesses in the eastern region reported a decline in input price, particularly for agriculture, industry, and mechanical services.[282] COVID-19 containment measures such as hand washing facilities, and social distancing have resulted in a slight increase in operating expenses for businesses. Overall, nine out of ten businesses have reportedly experienced an increase in operating expenses due to preventive measures instituted by the government to curb the spread of the virus. However, a majority of them (62%) reported an increase of less than 25%. Only 38% of the businesses reported an increase in operating costs of more than 25%. Businesses in the Central and Eastern regions experienced a slightly higher increment in the expenses with a majority of them quoting an increment of more than 25%. The hike in prices of hand washing facilities experienced at the onset of the pandemic in the country explains this.[283]

342. Approximately three-quarters of the surveyed businesses report a reduction in the number of employees. Overall, 76% of the businesses reported to have reduced the size of the workforce due to risk presented by COVID-19 and subsequent lockdown measures. Of these, 29% reduced their employees by more than 50%, and 27% of surveyed businesses reduced their employees by a range of 26%–50%. Only 21% of businesses reduced the workforce by a range of 1%–25%. Businesses in agriculture have undertaken the largest restructuring in the workforce, with 37% reducing their workforce by at least 50%, and another 44% by at least 26%. This is probably due to the severe decline in agricultural demand and revenues highlighted earlier. Similarly, a significantly high percentage of manufacturing businesses have laid off employees, with 41% reducing employees by more than 50%. Businesses in the Eastern region have undertaken the largest restructuring with more than 50% of them reducing their workforce by more than 50%. Similarly, a higher percentage of businesses in the Western, Northern, and Kampala reduced their workforce by more than 50%. On the other hand, businesses in the Central Uganda undertook a moderate restructuring of their workforce, with 41% reducing their workforce by a range of 26%–50%.[284]

343. The Ugandan government has continuously expected arriving passengers to hold a negative COVID-19 PCR test certificate issued within seventy-two hours from the time of sample collection to boarding aircraft leaving the country of origin.[285] Before departure from the country of origin to Entebbe International Airport, passengers are required to fill in an online health form that can be accessed on the

282. *Ibid.*
283. *Ibid.*
284. *Ibid.*
285. https://www.mofa.go.ug/data/dnews/727/COVID-19:%20TRAVELLING%20FROM%20AND%20TO%20UGANDA.html Accessed 28 Feb. 2022.

link https://arrivals.healthdesk.go.ug. The government also required mandatory testing on arrival at Entebbe International Airport for persons who are not fully vaccinated. From the customs area, passengers will exit the terminal to an arranged passenger holding area to wait for their PCR test results, which shall be availed after about two hours and thirty minutes or less. Effective 5 November 2021, all arriving passengers at Entebbe International Airport were to be allowed to go home after testing so that they self-isolate until their results are out. The positives would subsequently be tracked for further management according to the Ministry of Health's protocol for COVID-19.[286]

344. The then Chief Justice of the Republic of Uganda, his Lordship Bart M. Katureebe, issued guidelines for the operation of all courts in Uganda effective 20 March 2020.[287] For cases at the stage of submissions, the respective courts may advise the counsel/parties to file written submissions. During this time, prisoners and remandees will not be presented to the court. Where possible, proceedings may be conducted using a video link. All execution proceedings were suspended for the same period of time except where attachment had already taken place. Courts were to continue to handle certificates of urgency and take plea for serious cases and bail applications. Only the applicant and his/her lawyer, or in the case of bail application, the sureties will be allowed in the court. During this time, all judicial officers and staff will continue being on duty. However, there will be no open court appearances. Judicial officers shall use this period to complete pending judgments . Where possible judgments and rulings may be issued to the parties online or via e-mail. All conferences, workshops, meetings and local and foreign training programmes were suspended for a period of thirty-two days. Foreign travels for all judiciary staff save for exceptional circumstances were also suspended. In addition to the above guidelines, sanitizers and other preventive measures were also put in place. Digital thermometers are also being purchased and deployed at various court premises. Most of the guidelines are still operational to date.

345. The economic pain became severe as people were asked to stay at home, and the severity was felt in various sectors of the economy with travel bans affecting the aviation industry, sporting event cancellations affecting the sports industry, hospitality industry, financial sector, financial markets, events industry, entertainment industry, the prohibition of mass gatherings affecting the events and entertainment industries.[288]

---

286. https://www.mofa.go.ug/data/dnews/727/COVID-19:%20TRAVELLING%20FROM%20AND%20TO%20UGANDA.html Accessed 28 Feb. 2022.
287. https://www.loc.gov/item/global-legal-monitor/2020-04-29/uganda-government-measures-to-slow-the-spread-of-covid-19/ (Accessed 13 Mar. 2022).
288. Richard Wemesa, Christopher Wagima, Ivan Bakkaki, Dickson Turyareebahttps, The Economic Impact of the lockdown due to covid 19 pandemic on low income households of the five divisions of Kampala district in Uganda, www.scirp.org/journal/paperinformation.aspx?paperid=101421.

§2. Sports Associations' (Federations, Leagues, Clubs) Measures

346. Just like the government, the sports associations followed suit in the implementation of the standard operation procedures. Even other nations require negative PCR tests before granting entrance into their respective countries. Following the positive result for Lihanda, the 59 year old who was quarantined for two weeks following which he was expected to join up with the camp, Uganda's boxing federation president said his team was surprised that a member of the delegation had tested positive, given the measures in place. He further noted, '… We did Covid tests before travel and they returned negative, so as far as the Uganda environment is concerned we did everything possible … In Uganda, we tested them three times so it beats our understanding how this could have happened because he had been staying in camp with other athletes' Muhangi admitted that regulations could have been stricter as the boxing team prepared in camp for nearly two months in the Ugandan capital Kampala. 'We could have been more stringent because a camp should be non-accessible to outsiders,' he said. 'But when you have so many interests in the management of the team from the federation, the government and officials from the national Olympic committee and national sports council, that in a way could spark a challenge.' 'The boxers were meeting all sorts of people and I think we have learned a lesson that in future, a camp should be restricted for access save for those who have been authorised.'[289]

347. During the first wave of the pandemic, there was a rise in several unwanted situations, like an increase in teenage pregnancies, lack of employment among the youths, increased crime rates due. In order to overcome such circumstances, Uganda Tchoukball Association introduced weekly tchoukball trainings and coaching as a way to empower young girls to fight for their rights and freedoms, as well as use tchoukball sport as a tool for psycho-social support. Unfortunately, during the second wave, the Uganda Tchoukball Association like many other sports organizations had limited access to training fields, coupled with limited resources to extend support in kind to its players and young people. The fear of a third wave and limited capacities of international and government agencies were some of the factors responsible for deterring the provision of aid to the slum communities. Despite the challenging circumstances, Uganda Tchoukball Association was able to partner with other community interventions to create safer, sustainable places for slum girls and youth through the introduction of trainings in both soft and hard skills, as a way to make them economically independent. In order to make this happen, all the girls and youth were made to get a clear understanding on controlling and overcoming COVID-19.[290]

---

289. Tokyo 202: Second member of Uganda's Olympic delegation tests positive in Japan https://www.bbc.com/sport/africa/57579612 (accessed 2 Feb. 2022)
290. https://www.sportanddev.org/en/article/news/slum-youth-during-pandemic Accessed 1 Feb. 2022.

§3. CONCLUDING REMARKS

348. The lockdown weakened the performance of several sectors, dragging down national economic output. Among others, transport, accommodation, and food (hotels and restaurants), creative arts (entertainment), sports, and informal sectors seem to have been hit hardest by the recent lockdown.[291] Reliance on international rather than regional supply for raw materials and intermediates may be adversely affecting businesses in Uganda. This calls for firms, especially the micro and small companies, to explore the East African Community and COMESA market to get their supplies. In addition, the COVID-19 related risk is a clear opportunity for Uganda to develop a critical domestic value chains and supply chains so that businesses, particularly MSMEs, can have a stable source for their inputs, while saving on the scarce foreign exchange.

349. The government needs to consider one or a combination of the following: (i) tax rate reduction, (ii) reducing taxable income, (iii) offering tax credits, and (iv) offering tax refunds. Also, the government should pay all the outstanding arrears against supplies made to government. The government could also put in place or strengthen existing export financing and credit insurance mechanisms. Liquidity may prove insufficient should the COVID-19 crisis extend for more than two or three months.[292]

291. The socioeconomic impact of covid 19 on children https://www.unicef.org/uganda/media/10831/file/Impact%20of%20COVID-19%20on%20children%20in%20Uganda_01_13.09.2021.pdf (Accessed 13 Mar. 2022).
292. Corti Paul Lakuma et al., How has the COVID-19 Pandemic impacted Ugandan Businesses? Results from a business climate survey, Special issue No. 01 May, 2020.

Selected Bibliography

A. Books

Garner, Bryan A. *Black's Law Dictionary*. 2nd ed., 1995
Judicial Service Commission. *A Citizen's Handbook on Law & Administration of Justice in Uganda*. 3rd ed., 2007.
Weiler and Gary R. Roberts. *Sports and the Law*. 2nd ed., 1998, p. 240.

B. Reports/Articles

Aziz, Kitaka. Sports and the Law, 2019.
Davis, Timothy. What Is Sports Law? *Marquette Sports Law Review* 11, 2 (2021) spring.
Mukasa, Mulema. Impact of Sports Betting and Corruption: Reflections from Uganda, 29 November 2012.

C. Internet Sources

African Union Policy Framework for the Sustainable Development of Sport in Africa (2008–2018).
BBC News, *Uganda Country Profile*, 10 May 2018.
CCEDU: Labour Rights in Uganda.
Country Reports, Uganda Geography.
Daily Monitor, 'Stakeholders Want Sports Redefined' 25 May 2020 accessed 4 July 2021.
Daily Monitor, 'Tracing Uganda's Football history', 24 February 2017.
David Isabirye, 'Anti-doping in sports should be a brave, collective fight, says stakeholders'.
Federation of Uganda Football Associations.
Lakuma, Corti Paul et al., How has the COVID-19 Pandemic impacted Ugandan Businesses? Results from a business climate survey, Special issue No. 01 May 2020.
Parliament of Uganda, 'Speaker Calls for a bill on Compulsory Sports.' 28 June 2018 https://www.parliament.go.ug/news/2030/speaker-calls-bill-compulsory-sports
Richard Wemesa, Christopher Wagima, Ivan Bakkaki, Dickson Turyareebahttps, The Economic Impact of the lockdown due to covid 19 pandemic on low income households of the five divisions of Kampala district in Uganda

Selected Bibliography

The Observer, 'Museveni bans gambling, betting in Uganda'. 21 January 2019. https://observer.ug/news/headlines/59695-museveni-bans-gambling-betting-in-uganda

The Observer, 'Museveni bans gambling, betting in Uganda'. 21 January 2019. https://observer.ug/news/headlines/59695-museveni-bans-gambling-betting-in-uganda

Tokyo 202: Second member of Uganda's Olympic delegation tests positive in Japan https://www.bbc.com/sport/africa/57579612 (accessed on 2 February 2022).

Uganda Floorball Association gets global recognition, 25 March 2016. Available at: https://kawowo.com/2016/03/25/uganda-floorball-association-gets-global-recognition/.

Uganda Olympic Committee | Commonwealth Games Association Uganda. Available at http://nocuganda.org/about-us/.

Uganda Paralympic Committee Event Report Singapore 2019 World Para Swimming World Series 31 May 2019.

Youth Sports Uganda and their experiences of the pandemic. Available at: https://www.sportanddev.org/en/article/news/youth-sport-uganda-and-their-experiences-pandemic.

Index

The numbers here refer to paragraph numbers

Index

www.ingramcontent.com/pod-product-compliance
Ingram Content Group UK Ltd.
Pitfield, Milton Keynes, MK11 3LW, UK
UKHW020148290926
15471UKWH00004B/758